REGENTS HIGH SCHOOL MATHEMATICS B

EXAM REVIEW WORKBOOK

PARTS II, III, and IV

[Student Constructed Response Questions]

Anthony Nigro
Edwin Bernauer

© 2002

ISBN 0-937820-79-2
ISBN 0-937820-80-6 Ans. Key

REGENTS HIGH SCHOOL
MATHEMATICS B
EXAM REVIEW WORKBOOK
PARTS II, III, and IV

[Student Constructed Response Questions]

AUTHORS:

Anthony Nigro   Mathematics Teacher (Retired), Westbury High School
Co-author of Sequential Math I and III Workbooks
Co-author of Regents High School Mathematics A Workbook
Co-author of New York State Intermediate Math 8 Workbook

Edwin Bernauer   Mathematics Teacher, Westbury High School,
Co-Author of Sequential Math II and III Workbooks

WestSea Publishing Co., Inc.
149D Allen Boulevard
Farmingdale, NY 11735

(631) 420-1110 [Phone]
(631) 420-0754 [Fax]

ISBN 0-937820-79-2 [copyright 2002]
ISBN 0-937820-80-6 [Answer key]

INTRODUCTION

As was the case with our successful Regents High School **MATHEMATICS A** Examination Review Workbook, and the **INTERMEDIATE MATHEMATICS 8** Assessment Examination Workbook, this new **Regents High School MATHEMATICS B Examination Review Workbook, [Parts II, III, and IV Student Constructed Response Questions]**, is designed to prepare students for continuing to meet the New York State set of standards for Mathematics.

In using this **MATHEMATICS B Workbook, [Parts II, III, and IV Student Constructed Response Questions]**, the students will find helpful reminders and examples illustrating the required topics and problems. All are presented at the same level of difficulty and in the same format as New York State Regents High School **MATHEMATICS B Examination, parts II, III and IV.** In addition, wherever possible, problems have been constructed with relevant applications to reinforce the connection of mathematics to the real world. The student will also find problems more difficult in nature to encourage critical thinking and also to hone problem solving skills. Like the Regents High School **MATHEMATICS B** examination, it is assumed that the student is knowledgeable in the use of a *graphing calculator.*

Upon examining the Regents High School **MATHEMATICS B Workbook, parts II, III, and IV,** one will find that it contains the additions to Math Courses II, and III, such as:
1. Statistical problems (Confidence intervals, gathering data, appropriate displaying of data through curve fitting),
2. Probability problems (Bernoulli experiments and the relationship to the study of statistics and statistical inference including the use of normal curve).
3. Solving problems using the graphing calculator.

By using the **MATHEMATICS B workbook, parts II, III, IV, the seven "Key Ideas"** and the **MATHEMATICS B** Performance indicators outlined by the New York State Education Department have been thoroughly addressed.

Also included in this **MATHEMATICS B Workbook, parts II, III, IV** is a **Westsea MATHEMATICS B** Practice Regents Examination consisting of four parts:

Part I	20 multiple-choice questions	[40 credits]
Part II	6 short student constructed response questions	[12 credits]
Part III	6 extended student constructed response questions	[24 credits]
Part IV	2 extended student constructed response questions	[12 credits]

A scoring key for part I and Holistic Rubrics for parts II, III, and IV is included in a *separate* answer booklet that is available to teachers.

The maximum total credits for the **MATHEMATICS B** Regents Examination add up to 88.

Also available is the **Regents High School MATHEMATICS B Examination Review workbook, [Part I Multiple-Choice Questions].**

We at WestSea are proud of all our publications that were designed to help students meet the challenge of higher academic standards and to pass the required assessments that evolved as a result of these standards. We are confident that our newest publications will again contribute to student success.

REGENTS HIGH SCHOOL
MATHEMATICS B
EXAM REVIEW WORKBOOK
PARTS II, III, and IV

[Student Constructed Response Questions]

TABLE OF CONTENTS

UNIT 1 MATHEMATICAL REASONING

TABLE OF CONTENTS (CONTINUED)

UNIT 2 NUMBER and NUMERATION (Continued)

UNIT 3 OPERATIONS

TABLE OF CONTENTS (CONTINUED)

UNIT 3 OPERATIONS (Continued)

UNIT 4 MODELING/MULTIPLE REPRESENTATION

TABLE OF CONTENTS (CONTINUED)

UNIT 4 MODELING/MULTIPLE REPRESENTATION (Continued)

UNIT 5 MEASUREMENT

UNIT 6 UNCERTAINTY

TABLE OF CONTENTS (CONTINUED)

UNIT 6 UNCERTAINTY (Continued)

UNIT 7 PATTERNS/FUNCTIONS

REGENTS HIGH SCHOOL
MATHEMATICS B

EXAM REVIEW WORKBOOK
PARTS II, III, AND IV

[Student Constructed Response Questions]

UNIT 1
MATHEMATICAL REASONING

Euclidean direct proofs based on deductive reasoning

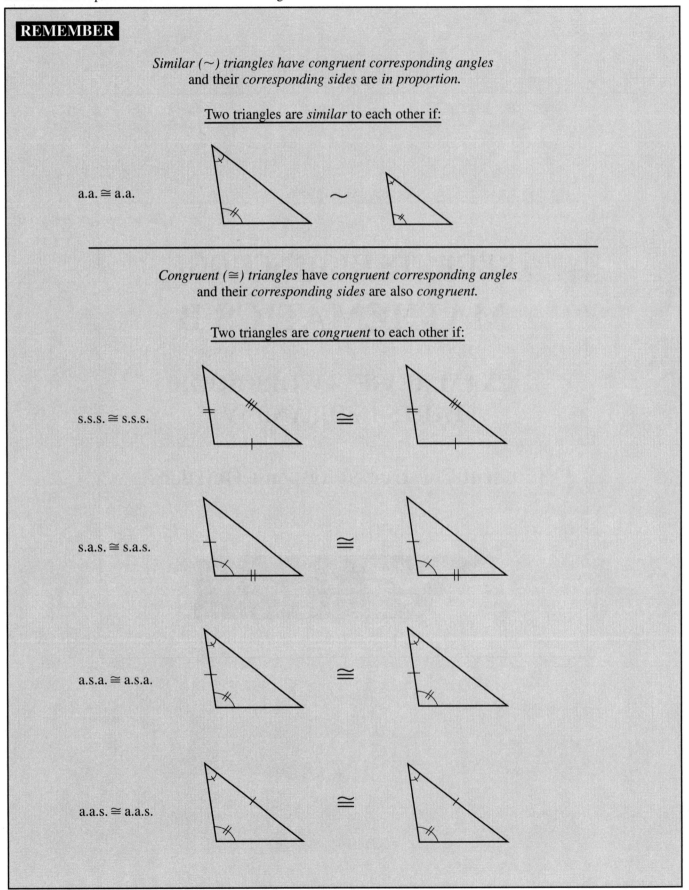

REMEMBER

Similar (~) triangles have congruent corresponding angles
and their *corresponding sides* are *in proportion.*

Two triangles are *similar* to each other if:

a.a. ≅ a.a.   ~

_____

Congruent (≅) triangles have *congruent corresponding angles*
and their *corresponding sides* are also *congruent.*

Two triangles are *congruent* to each other if:

s.s.s. ≅ s.s.s.   ≅

s.a.s. ≅ s.a.s.   ≅

a.s.a. ≅ a.s.a.   ≅

a.a.s. ≅ a.a.s.   ≅

UNIT 1
MATHEMATICAL REASONING

Euclidean direct proofs based on deductive reasoning (continued)

REMEMBER

Two *right* triangles are *congruent* to each other if:

Hyp Leg ≅ Hyp Leg 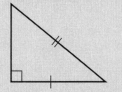 ≅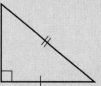

REMEMBER

Example:

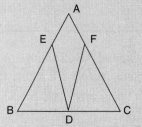

Given: △ABC, $\overline{AEB}$, $\overline{AFC}$, D is the midpoint of $\overline{BC}$,
$\overline{ED} \cong \overline{FD}$, ∠EDC ≅ ∠FDB.

Prove: △ABC is isosceles.

Solution:

Statements	Reasons
1. △ABC, $\overline{AEB}$, $\overline{AFC}$, D is the midpoint of $\overline{BC}$.	1. Given.
2. $\overline{BD} \cong \overline{DC}$.	2. Definition of a midpoint.
3. $\overline{ED} \cong \overline{FD}$.	3. Given.
4. ∠EDF ≅ ∠EDF.	4. Reflexive property of congruence.
5. ∠EDC ≅ ∠FDB.	5. Given.
6. ∠EDC - ∠EDF ≅ ∠FDB - ∠EDF or ∠EDB ≅ ∠FDC.	6. Subtraction postulate of congruent angles.
7. △EDB ≅ △FDC.	7. s.a.s. ≅ s.a.s. (steps 2, 3 and 6).
8. ∠B ≅ ∠C.	8. Corresponding angles of congruent triangles are congruent.
9. $\overline{AB} \cong \overline{AC}$.	9. If two angles of a triangle are congruent then the sides opposite these angles are congruent.
10. △ABC is isosceles.	10. Definition of an isosceles triangles.

UNIT 1
MATHEMATICAL REASONING

Euclidean direct proofs based on deductive reasoning (continued)

1. Given: $\triangle$ABC, $\overline{BEA} \cong \overline{BDC}$, $\overline{AD}$ and $\overline{CE}$
intersect at F, and $\angle$FAC $\cong \angle$FCA.

   Prove: $\overline{FE} \cong \overline{FD}$.

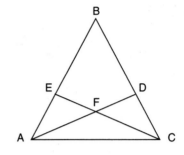

2. Given: quadrilateral ABCD with
diagonals $\overline{AEFC}$, $\overline{DE} \perp \overline{AC}$, $\overline{BF} \perp \overline{AC}$,
$\angle$EDC $\cong \angle$ABF, $\overline{AE} \cong \overline{BF}$.

   Prove: ABCD is a parallelogram.

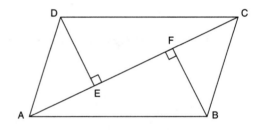

3. Given: Parallelogram GHIJ
with diagonals $\overline{GI}$ and
$\overline{JH}$ meeting at point K.

   Prove: The diagonals bisect each other.

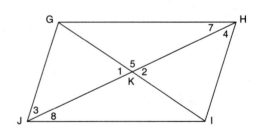

4

UNIT 1
MATHEMATICAL REASONING

Euclidean direct proofs based on deductive reasoning (continued)

REMEMBER

Example:

Given: ABCD is a parallelogram,
$\overline{ADE}$ and $\overline{BFE}$.

Prove: a $\triangle$ BCF ~ $\triangle$ EDF

b $\dfrac{\overline{BC}}{\overline{DE}} = \dfrac{\overline{BF}}{\overline{FE}}$

c $(\overline{BC})(\overline{FE}) = (\overline{DE})(\overline{BF})$

d $\dfrac{\overline{AD}}{\overline{DE}} = \dfrac{\overline{BF}}{\overline{FE}}$

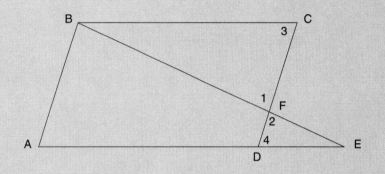

Solution:

Statements	Reasons
1. ▱ABCD, segments ADE and BFE.	1. Given.
2. $\angle 1 \cong \angle 2$	2. Vertical angles are congruent.
3. $\overline{BC} \parallel \overline{AD}$	3. Opposite sides of a ▱ are ∥.
4. $\angle 3 \cong \angle 4$	4. If 2 ∥ lines are cut by a transversal, the alternative interior angles are ≅.
5. $\triangle$BCF ~ $\triangle$EDF	5. AA ≅ AA.
6. $\dfrac{\overline{BC}}{\overline{DE}} = \dfrac{\overline{BF}}{\overline{FE}}$	6. In similar triangles, corresponding sides are in proportion.
7. $(\overline{BC})(\overline{FE}) = (\overline{DE})(\overline{BF})$	7. In a proportion, the product of the means = the product of the extremes.
8. $\overline{BC} \cong \overline{AD}$	8. Opposite sides of a ▱ are ≅.
9. $\dfrac{\overline{AD}}{\overline{DE}} = \dfrac{\overline{BF}}{\overline{FE}}$	9. Substitution.

5

Euclidean direct proofs based on deductive reasoning (continued)

1. Given: △ABC, altitudes $\overline{BE}$ and $\overline{AD}$
   are drawn.

   Prove: *a* △BEC ~ △ADC

       b $\overline{BC} : \overline{AC} = \overline{BE} : \overline{AD}$

       c $\overline{AC} \times \overline{BE} = \overline{BC} \times \overline{AD}$

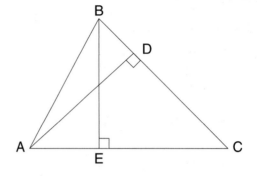

UNIT 1
MATHEMATICAL REASONING

Euclidean direct proofs based on deductive reasoning (continued)

2. Given: Chords $\overline{AB}$ and $\overline{CD}$ in circle O intersect at an interior point E.

   Chords $\overline{AD}$ and $\overline{CB}$ are drawn.

Prove: *a* $\triangle$ AED ~ $\triangle$BEC

   b $\dfrac{\overline{AE}}{\overline{CE}} = \dfrac{\overline{ED}}{\overline{EB}}$

   c (AE)(EB) = (CE)(ED)

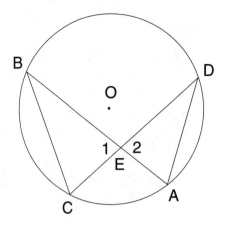

UNIT 1
MATHEMATICAL REASONING

Analytic direct proofs based on deductive reasoning.

REMEMBER

Example:

I. Quadrilateral ABCD has coordinates A (-3, 2), B (2, 5), C (3, 1), and D (-2, -2). Using coordinate geometry, prove that

    a the diagonals bisect each other
    b the opposite sides are congruent
    c the opposite sides are parallel

II. Give a reason why the quadrilateral ABCD is a parallelogram.

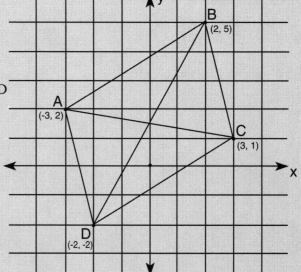

Solution:

a Plot the points A, B, C, D on graph paper. If the diagonals bisect each other they would have the same midpoint. Find the midpoints of diagonals $\overline{AC}$ & $\overline{BD}$.

Midpoint of $\overline{AC} = \left(\dfrac{x_1 + x_2}{2}, \dfrac{y_1 + y_2}{2} \right)$

Midpoint of $\overline{AC} = \left(\dfrac{-3 + 3}{2}, \dfrac{2 + 1}{2} \right)$

Midpoint of $\overline{AC} = \left(0, \dfrac{3}{2} \right)$

Midpoint of $\overline{BD} = \left(\dfrac{2 - 2}{2}, \dfrac{5 - 2}{2} \right)$

Midpoint of $\overline{BD} = \left(0, \dfrac{3}{2} \right)$

Since the midpoints of $\overline{AC}$ & $\overline{BD}$ are the same, the lines bisect each other.

Analytic direct proofs based on deductive reasoning (continued).

b Use the distance formula to show that
$\overline{AD} \cong \overline{BC}$ and $\overline{DC} \cong \overline{AB}$.

$$d = \sqrt{(x_2 - x_1)^2 + (y_2 - y_1)^2}$$

$AD = \sqrt{(-3 + 2)^2 + (2 + 2)^2}$ $AB = \sqrt{(-3 - 2)^2 + (2 - 5)^2}$

$AD = \sqrt{(-1)^2 + (4)^2}$ $AB = \sqrt{(-5)^2 + (-3)^2}$

$AD = \sqrt{1 + 16}$ $AB = \sqrt{25 + 9}$

$AD = \sqrt{17}$ $AB = \sqrt{34}$

$BC = \sqrt{(2 - 3)^2 + (5 - 1)^2}$ $CD = \sqrt{(3 + 2)^2 + (1 + 2)^2}$

$BC = \sqrt{(-1)^2 + (4)^2}$ $CD = \sqrt{(5)^2 + (3)^2}$

$BC = \sqrt{1 + 16}$ $CD = \sqrt{25 + 9}$

$BC = \sqrt{17}$ $CD = \sqrt{34}$

$\overline{AD} \cong \overline{BC}$ $\overline{AB} \cong \overline{CD}$

c Use the slope formula to show that the slopes of the opposite sides are equal. Then the opposite sides will be parallel.

$\text{Slope } \overline{AB} = \dfrac{y_2 - y_1}{x_2 - x_1} = \dfrac{5 - 2}{2 + 3} = \dfrac{3}{5}$ $\text{Slope } \overline{DC} = \dfrac{-2 - 1}{-2 - 3} = \dfrac{3}{5}$

$\text{Slope } \overline{AD} = \dfrac{2 + 2}{-3 + 2} = -4$ $\text{Slope } \overline{BC} = \dfrac{5 - 1}{2 - 3} = -4$

Since the opposite sides have the same slope, they are parallel to each other.

II. Any one of the three proofs above, *a*, *b*, or *c*, show a quadrilateral is a parallelogram.

UNIT 1
MATHEMATICAL REASONING

Analytic direct proofs based on deductive reasoning (continued).

1. Given E(0, 5), F(6, 8), G(12, 5) and H(2, 0)
   Prove: Quadrilateral EFGH ia a trapezoid.
   [*The use of the accompanying grid is optional.*]

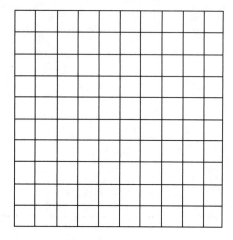

2. The vertices of triangles IJK are I(0, 0), J(2a, 2b), and K(2c, 2d). Using the methods of coordinate geometry, show that the line joining the midpoints of $\overline{IK}$ and $\overline{JK}$ is parallel to line I J.

3. The vertices of quadrilateral LMNP are L(0, 0), M (2a, 0), N(2b, 2c), and P(2d, 2e).
   Points Q, R, S, and T are the midpoints of $\overline{LM}$, $\overline{MN}$, $\overline{NP}$, and $\overline{PL}$, respectively.
   a Using the coordinates of L, M, N, and P, show how you can express the coordinates of the midpoints Q, R, S, and T in terms of the variables *a, b, c, d*, and *e*.
   b Show and explain why $\overline{QR} \parallel \overline{ST}$ and $\overline{QT} \parallel \overline{RS}$.

UNIT 1
MATHEMATICAL REASONING

Analytic direct proofs based on deductive reasoning (continued).

4. If parallelogram UVWZ is the *XY*-plane and the coordinates of its vertices are U(0, 0), V(a, 0), W($a + b, c$) and Z(b, c), show why the opposite sides of parallelogram UVWZ are congruent.

5. Quadrilateral ABCD has coordinates A(0, 5a), B(3a, 5a), C(4a, 0), and D(-a, 0). Prove by coordinate geometry that quadrilateral ABCD is an isosceles trapezoid.

6. The vertices of quadrilateral EFGH are E(a, 2b), F(4a, 4b), G(9a, 4b), and H(6a, 2b).
   - a Using coordinate geometry, express in terms of a and b the length of each side of quadrilateral EFGH.
   - b If $a = 1$ and $b = 2$, find the lengths of $\overline{MN}$ and $\overline{MR}$

UNIT 1
MATHEMATICAL REASONING

Euclidean indirect proofs based on deductive reasoning

REMEMBER

Example:

Given: Given trapezoid TONY with diagonals $\overline{TN}$ and $\overline{YO}$ intersecting at point X, prove that the diagonals of the trapezoid do *not* bisect each other.

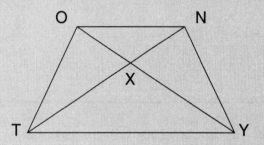

Solution:

Statements	Reasons
1. Trapezoid TONY with diagonals $\overline{TN}$ and $\overline{YO}$	1. Given.
2. $\overline{ON} \parallel \overline{TY}$	2. A trapezoid ia a quadrilateral with 1 and only 1 pair of parallel sides.
3. If we assume diagonals bisect each other, then $\overline{TX} \cong \overline{XN}$, and $\overline{OX} \cong \overline{YX}$	3. Definition of a bisector of a segment.
4. $\angle TXO \cong \angle YXN$	4. When 2 lines intersect, the vertical angles are $\cong$.
5. $\triangle TXO \cong \triangle YXN$	5. SAS $\cong$ SAS
6. $\angle OTX \cong \angle YNX$	6. CPCTC
7. $\overline{OT} \parallel \overline{NY}$	7. If 2 lines are cut by a transversal and the alternate interior angles are congruent, the lines are parallel.
8. $\overline{OT} \nparallel \overline{NY}$	8. Contradiction by definition of a trapezoid. A trapezoid has only 1 pair of $\parallel$ sides.
9. The diagonals do not bisect each other	9. A trapezoid is not a subset of a parallelogram.

UNIT 1
MATHEMATICAL REASONING

Euclidean indirect proofs based on deductive reasoning (continued)

1. Use the indirect method of proof. Angle ABC is an acute angle inscribed in circle O. P is a point so located that $m\angle APC < m\angle B$. Prove that point P must be *outside* circle O.

2. In $\triangle$ ABC, $\overline{AB} \cong \overline{AC}$. $\overleftrightarrow{AC}$ is extended through C to point E and $\overline{AB}$ is extended through B to point D so that $\overline{BD} > \overline{CE}$. Line DE is drawn. Prove that $m\angle E > m\angle D$.

3. In parallelogram ABCD, $\overline{AD} > \overline{DC}$ and diagonal $\overline{AC}$ is drawn. Prove that $\overline{AC}$ does *not* bisect $\angle BCD$.

4. The bisector of $\angle BAC$ of $\triangle$ ABC intersects $\overline{BC}$ at point D.
   Prove: *a* $m\angle ADC > m\angle DAC$
           b $\overline{AC} > \overline{DC}$

UNIT 1
MATHEMATICAL REASONING

Euclidean indirect proofs based on deductive reasoning (continued)

5. In an acute △ABC, the altitude from vertex B meets side $\overline{AC}$ at point D.
   If $m\angle ABD > m\angle CBD$, prove that $\overline{AB} > \overline{BC}$.

6. Using the indirect method, prove that in △ABC, if side $\overline{AC}$ is *not* equal to side $\overline{BC}$, then the median $\overline{CD}$ to side $\overline{AB}$ is *not* ⊥ $\overline{AB}$.

7. Given line $\overleftrightarrow{AB}$ is *not* parallel to line $\overleftrightarrow{CD}$ and $\overline{AB} \cong \overline{AC}$.
   Prove $m\angle 1 \neq m\angle 2$.

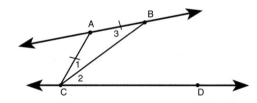

UNIT 1
MATHEMATICAL REASONING

Indirect reasoning in everyday situations

1. Albert's upholstery store has three ranges of prices for repairs. Show how labor and material can effect which price range is used.

2. Bob has bowling shoes, tennis sneakers, and football cleats in an unlit closet. Show how he can pick out any one type of footwear without the use of any light.

3. The coach of the varsity high school baseball team will be late for the start of the baseball game. He informs the assistant coach that the starting pitcher should be either Cal, Don or Ed. The coach arrives at the game after the first two, pitches are thrown by his teams pitcher. He notices that Cal and Don are in the dugout. Prove that the coach knows that the assistant coach selected Ed to be the starting pitcher.

4. Frances has not decided whether she will attend the high school prom with a date, go to a beach party with her friends, or stay home and read a book. George goes to the high school prom and does not see Frances there. The weather is very overcast and heavy rain is forecast. Give two possible explanations on what decision Frances could have made.

UNIT 1
MATHEMATICAL REASONING

5. Henry was watching a baseball game on his TV. His family is a cable customer. Just as the batter swung at the ball, the sound and the picture on his TV went blank. Explain how Henry can decide if the cable failed, the TV failed, or the circuit breaker opened and stopped the flow of electricity.

6. A drug company has submitted a certain drug for approval in curing a certain illness. If this drug is approved, the drug company can earn an additional 50 million dollars. The drug company recalls the submission for approval with the excuse that it would like to also test the drug as a cure for a secondary illness. The use of this drug for the secondary illness would add an additional 100,000 dollars to its earnings. By recalling the submission of approval, there could be an additional 3 year delay in final approval. Using indirect reasoning, what conclusion can you reach regarding the actual reason for the drug company recall of the original submission for approval?

7. Jack's diner has a daily special of Appetizer (Seafood Bisque), Entree (Roast Prime Rib of Beef), Dessert (Cheese Cake), and Drink (Coffee). Karen has the prices $1.50, $3.25, $4.50, and $10.95. Explain how she should match up the prices with the food items.

UNIT 2
NUMBER AND NUMERATION

Understand and use rational and irrational numbers

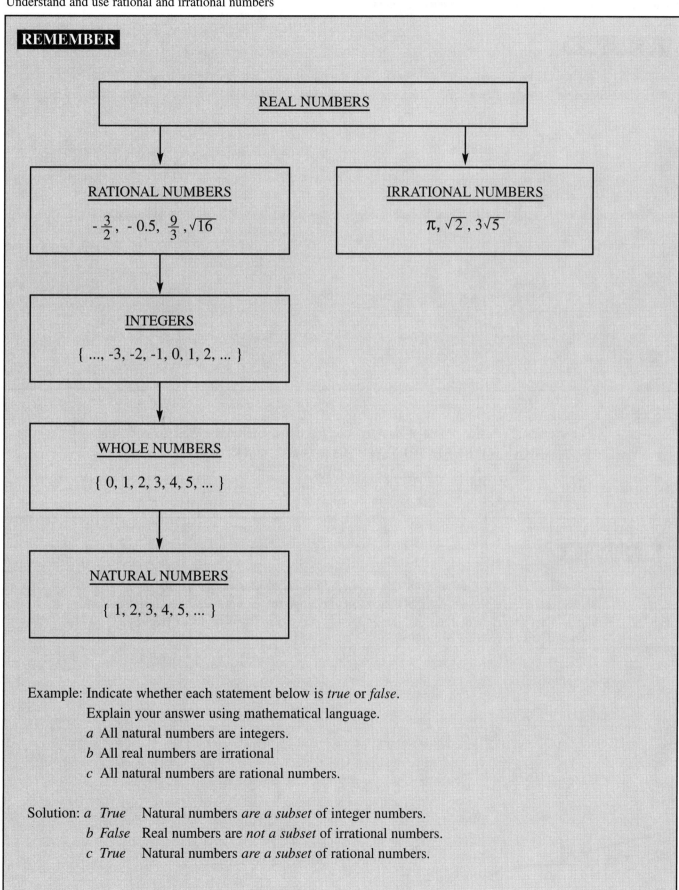

REMEMBER

REAL NUMBERS

RATIONAL NUMBERS

$-\frac{3}{2}$, -0.5, $\frac{9}{3}$, $\sqrt{16}$

IRRATIONAL NUMBERS

π, $\sqrt{2}$, $3\sqrt{5}$

INTEGERS

{ ..., -3, -2, -1, 0, 1, 2, ... }

WHOLE NUMBERS

{ 0, 1, 2, 3, 4, 5, ... }

NATURAL NUMBERS

{ 1, 2, 3, 4, 5, ... }

Example: Indicate whether each statement below is *true* or *false*.

Explain your answer using mathematical language.

a All natural numbers are integers.

b All real numbers are irrational

c All natural numbers are rational numbers.

Solution: *a True* Natural numbers *are a subset* of integer numbers.

b False Real numbers are *not a subset* of irrational numbers.

c True Natural numbers *are a subset* of rational numbers.

UNIT 2
NUMBER AND NUMERATION

Understand and use rational and irrational numbers (continued)

REMEMBER

A fraction is undefined or meaningless when the *denominator* is equal to zero.

Example: Which value(s) of x cause the function to be undefined?

$$f(x) = \frac{(x + 6)(x - 2)}{x^2 - 2x - 15}$$

Solution: Set the denominator = 0 $x^2 - 2x - 15 = 0$

         Solve for the value(s) of x $(x - 5)(x + 3) = 0$

$$x - 5 = 0 \quad \text{or} \quad x + 3 = 0$$
$$x = 5 \quad \text{or} \quad x = -3$$

         The fraction is indefined when $x = 5$ or $x = -3$

For additional practice problems on Algebraic fractions, refer to the Westsea Publishing
SEQUENTIAL MATHEMATICS 3 Regents Exam Review Workbook
pages 2 to 6, and 101, 102, 140.

REMEMBER

To Simplify complex fractions, find the least common denominator, [LCD] for all the fractions. Use the distributive property of multiplication to change the complex fraction into a factorable fraction. Factor both numerator and denominator and reduce to a simplified fraction.

Example 1: Express in *simplest* form:

$$\frac{1 + \dfrac{2}{x - 1}}{2 - \dfrac{x - 3}{x - 1}}$$

Solution 1: Multiply both numerator and denominator by the LCD, $(x - 1)$.

$$\frac{(x - 1) + 2}{2(x - 1) - (x - 3)} = \frac{x + 1}{2x - 2 - x + 3} = \frac{x + 1}{x + 1} = 1$$

REMEMBER

Simplifying complex fractions (continued)

Example 2:   Simplify *completely*:

$$1 - \frac{1}{1 + \dfrac{n}{1-n}}$$

Solution 2:   Multiply both the numerator and denominator of the complex part *only* by the LCD, $(1 - n)$.

$$1 - \frac{1}{\dfrac{1(1-n)}{(1-n)} + \dfrac{n(1-n)}{(1-n)(1-n)}} \quad = \quad 1 - \frac{1}{\dfrac{(1-n)}{(1-n)} + \dfrac{n}{(1-n)}}$$

$$1 - \frac{1}{\dfrac{1-n+n}{(1-n)}} \quad = \quad 1 - \frac{1}{\dfrac{1}{(1-n)}} \quad = \quad 1 - (1-n) = n$$

1. Simplify the above problem in the REMEMBER statement by multiplying the problems's numerator and denominator by the LCD, $(1 - n)$

For additional practice problems on Complex fractions, refer to the Westsea Publishing
SEQUENTIAL MATHEMATICS 3 Regents Exam Review Workbook page 5.

UNIT 2
NUMBER AND NUMERATION

Understand and use rational and irrational numbers (continued)

REMEMBER

REMEMBER

An expression must be simplified when there is a radical term in the denominator.

Example: $\dfrac{3}{6 - 5\sqrt{2}}$

Solution: $\dfrac{3}{(6 - 5\sqrt{2})} \cdot \dfrac{(6 + 5\sqrt{2})}{(6 + 5\sqrt{2})}$ Multiply numerator and denominator by the conjugate of the denominator.

$\dfrac{18 + 15\sqrt{2}}{36 + 30\sqrt{2} - 30\sqrt{2} - (25)(2)}$ Use the distributative property. Use the F.O.I.L. method.

$\dfrac{18 + 15\sqrt{2}}{-14} = \dfrac{-18 - 15\sqrt{2}}{14}$ Simplify

---

1. Express $\dfrac{\sqrt{3}}{\dfrac{1}{\sqrt{3}} + 1}$ as a number in the form $a + b\sqrt{3}$, where a and b are integers.

For additional practice problems on Irrational denominators, refer to Westsea Publishing
SEQUENTIAL MATHEMATICS 3 Regents Exam Review Workbook pages 9 and 10.

REMEMBER

To reduce a fraction containing polynomials, factor completely first. Then divide both numerator and denominator by the greatest common factor, [GCF]

Example: Reduce $\dfrac{6x^2 + 12x}{x^3 - 5x^2 - 14x}$

Solution: $\dfrac{6x(x + 2)}{x(x^2 - 5x - 14)} = \dfrac{6(x + 2)}{x^2 - 5x - 14} = \dfrac{6(x + 2)}{(x + 2)(x - 7)} = \dfrac{6}{x - 7}$

---

1. Simplify

$$\dfrac{5x^3 - 25x^2 - 30x}{x^2 - 5x - 6}$$

UNIT 2
NUMBER AND NUMERATION

Recogonize the order of the real numbers

Example 1: Arrange the numbers in the set below from lowest value to highest value.

$$3.\overline{76}, \qquad 3.7\overline{6}, \qquad 3.7, \qquad 3.76, \qquad 3.\overline{7}$$

Solution 1: 3.7676..., 3.7666..., 3.7000, 3.7600, 3.7777... [shown 4 dec places]

Now put in order from lowest to highest value.

3.700   3.7600   3.7666...   3.7676...   3.7777...

Now rewrite as given in the example.

3.7 3.76 $3.7\overline{6}$ $3.\overline{76}$ $3.\overline{7}$ answer

Example 2: Arrange the numbers in the set below from highest value to lowest value.

$$6.238 \qquad 6.\overline{238} \qquad 6.2\overline{38} \qquad 6.23\overline{8}$$

Solution 2: 6.238000   6.238238...   6.238383...   6.238888...   [6 dec places]

Now put in order from highest value to lowest value.

6.238888...   6.238383...   6.238238...   6.238000

Now rewrite as given in the example.

$6.23\overline{8}$ $6.2\overline{38}$ $6.\overline{238}$ 6.238 answer

1. Arrange the numbers in the set below from smallest to largest.

$$9.8 \qquad 9.85 \qquad 9.8\overline{5} \qquad 9.\overline{85} \qquad 9.\overline{8}$$

UNIT 2
NUMBER AND NUMERATION

Apply properties of the real numbers to various subsets of numbers

Examples: Express each of the repeating decimals as common fractions.

a $16.9\overline{5}$ b $16.\overline{95}$ c $7.\overline{4}$ d $0.\overline{6}$ e $-0.0\overline{351}$

Solutions: a $10n = 169.5555...$ b $100n = 1695.9595...$
$$\frac{\begin{array}{r} n = 16.9555... \end{array}}{9n = 152.600}$$
$$\frac{\begin{array}{r} n = 16.9595... \end{array}}{99n = 1679.0000}$$

$$n = \frac{763}{45}$$ $$n = \frac{1679}{99}$$

c $10n = 74.44...$ d $10n = 6.66...$ e $1000n = -35.1351351...$
$$\frac{\begin{array}{r} n = 7.44... \end{array}}{9n = 67.00}$$
$$\frac{\begin{array}{r} n = 0.66... \end{array}}{9n = 6.00}$$
$$\frac{\begin{array}{r} n = -0.0351351... \end{array}}{999n = -35.1}$$

$$n = \frac{67}{9}$$ $$n = \frac{6}{9} = \frac{2}{3}$$ $$n = \frac{-35.1}{999} = \frac{-13}{370}$$

An *alternative method* is to treat the repeating decimal as the <u>Sum of a geometric series</u> using the formula:
$$S = \frac{a}{1-r}$$ where a is the 1st term of the series, r is the common ratio.

Lets try problem d above where $n = 0.\overline{6} = 0.66666...$

$S = 0.6 + 0.06 + 0.006 + ...$ The 1st term is $a = 0.6$ The common ratio is $r = \dfrac{0.06}{0.6} = 0.1$

$$S = \frac{a}{1-r} = \frac{0.6}{1.0 - 0.1} = \frac{0.6}{0.9} = \frac{2}{3}$$ [note that this is the same answer as above]

---

1. Express as a common fraction: a $0.3\overline{5}$ b $0.2\overline{3}$ c $0.\overline{63}$

   Use both methods in the REMEMBER statement above and compare answers.

UNIT 2
NUMBER AND NUMERATION

Apply properties of the real numbers to various subsets of numbers (continued)

REMEMBER

Rational integral functions of x

an **integral function** of x does *not* have x in the <u>denominator</u> nor x with a *negative exponent* in the <u>numerator</u>.

For example:

$$\frac{2}{x} \qquad\qquad \frac{x+1}{x^2} \qquad\qquad x^{-2}$$

A **rational function** of x does *not* contain x <u>under a radical sign</u> nor x with a <u>*fractional exponent.*</u>

For example:

$$\sqrt{x} \qquad\qquad x^{\frac{1}{3}} \qquad\qquad \sqrt[3]{5x}$$

Example: Which of the following is a rational integral function of x? Explain your answer.

(1) $x^{\frac{4}{3}} + x - 5$ (3) $-5x^2 + 3x - 15$

(2) $3x^{-3} + 4x - 2$ (4) $3x^2 + 2x\sqrt{x} - x + 4$

Solution: (1) is *not rational* because of $x^{\frac{4}{3}}$

(2) is *not integral* because of x^{-3}

(3) answer   A rational integral function of x: ans (3)

(4) is *not rational* because of $\sqrt{x}$

---

1. Which of the following is a rational integral function of x? Explain your answer.

(1) $2x^6 + 3$ (3) $4 - x^{-2}$

(2) $3x^{\frac{2}{5}} - 1$ (4) $8\sqrt[3]{x} + 1$

UNIT 2
NUMBER AND NUMERATION

Apply properties of the real numbers to various subsets of numbers (continued)

---

2. Which of the following is a rational integral function of x? Explain your answer.

(1) $2x^2 - \sqrt{x} - 1$

(3) $x^2 - \dfrac{3}{x} - 5$

(2) $\dfrac{2}{3}x^2 + 4x - 6$

(4) $x^{\frac{2}{3}} - x - 5$

---

3. Which of the following is a rational integral function of x? Explain your answer.

(1) $x + \dfrac{1}{x}$

(3) $x^2 + x^{\frac{3}{2}}$

(2) $\sqrt{x + 3}$

(4) $x + 4^{\frac{1}{2}}$

---

4. Which of the following is a rational integral function of x? Explain your answer.

(1) $x^{\frac{2}{3}}$

(3) $x^{-\frac{5}{2}}$

(2) $\sqrt{7x - 1}$

(4) $-5x^3$

---

5. if r is a positive real number and n is a positive integer, then $r^{-\frac{1}{n}}$ is equivalent to:

(1) $\dfrac{1}{r^{-n}}$

(3) $\sqrt[n]{r}$

(2) $\dfrac{1}{\sqrt[n]{r}}$

(4) r^n

24

Apply properties of the real numbers to various subsets of numbers (continued)

6. Show whether the following statement is true or false for all *real* numbers of x.

$$|x| = \sqrt[3]{x^3}$$

7. Show whether the following statement is true or false for all *real* numbers of x.

$$x = \sqrt[3]{x^3}$$

8. Show whether the following statement is true or false for all *real* numbers of x.

$$|x - 2| < 0$$

9. Show whether the following statement is true or false for all *real* numbers of x.

$$|x - 2| > 0$$

10. Show whether the following statement is true or false for all *real* numbers of x.

$$|x - 2| > (x - 2)$$

UNIT 2
NUMBER AND NUMERATION

Apply properties of the real numbers to various subsets of numbers (continued)

REMEMBER

If *a, b,* and *c* represent real numbers, then

$(a + b) + c = a + (b + c)$ [*associative* property of addition]

$(ab)c = a(bc)$ [*associative* property of multiplication]

$a + b = b + a$ [*commutative* property of addition]

$ab = ba$ [*commutative* property of multiplication]

$a(b + c) = ab + ac$ [*distributive* property of multiplication]

$a + (-a) = 0, (-a) + a = 0$ [additive *inverse*]

$a \cdot \dfrac{1}{a} = 1, \quad \dfrac{1}{a} \cdot a = 1$ [multiplicative *inverse*]

$a + 0 = a, \qquad 0 + a = a$ [0, the *identity element* for addition]

$a \cdot 1 = a, \qquad 1 \cdot a = a$ [1, *identity element* for multiplication]

$a \cdot 0 = 0, \qquad 0 \cdot a = 0$ [multiplication *property of zero*]

Example: Indicate whether each statement below is *true* or *false*. Use $a = 10$, $b = 3$, $c = 1$.

associative property of *addition*	associative property of *subtraction*	associative property of *multiplication*
$(a + b) + c = a + (b + c)$	$(a - b) - c = a - (b - c)$	$(ab)c = a(bc)$

Solution:

$(10 + 3) + 1 = 10 + (3 + 1)$	$(10 - 3) - 1 = 10 - (3 - 1)$	$(10 \cdot 3)1 = 10(3 \cdot 1)$
$13 + 1 = 10 + 4$	$7 - 1 = 10 - 2$	$(30)1 = 10 (3)$
$14 = 14$ *True*	$6 \neq 8$ *False*	$30 = 30$ *True*

Therefore, there is no associative property of subtraction.
Lets confirm this by using the variables *a, b,* and *c.*

$$(a - b) - c = a - (b - c)$$

$$a - b - c = a - b + c$$

$$- c \neq c \qquad \text{where } c \neq 0$$

26

UNIT 2
NUMBER AND NUMERATION

Apply properties of the real numbers to various subsets of numbers (continued)

The distance between the columns of the Parthenon in Athens, Greece and the height of the vertical columns make up a rectangle known as the golden rectangle. Here the ratio for length to width is approximately 1.61803... . This ratio, the golden ratio, has been considered to be the most pleasing to the eye. The golden ratio states that a number is equal to its reciprocal plus one.

Say the number is represented by the length, L, of a rectangle divided by its width, W, then

$$\frac{L}{W} = \frac{W}{L} + 1 \qquad \text{or} \qquad \frac{W}{L} \cdot \frac{L}{L} \qquad \text{or} \qquad \frac{W + L}{L}$$

$$\frac{L}{W} = \frac{W + L}{L} \qquad \text{or} \qquad L^2 = W(W + L) \qquad \text{or} \qquad L^2 = W^2 + WL$$

Example 1: A graphing calculator is 3.25 inches in width and 7.25 inches in length.

Does the shape of the graphing calculator appear to be a golden rectangle?

Solution 1: $\frac{L}{W} = \frac{7.25}{3.25} = 2.23$ 2.23:1 is a much larger ratio than 1.61083:1

---

1. A scientific calculator is 5.25 inches high and 3.0 inches wide. Is it within 10% of the requirements for a golden rectangle? Show your calculations.

---

2. A credit card is 3.375 inches by 2.125 inches. Show your calculations to prove whether the credit card is a golden rectangle.

---

3. An 8.5 by 11 inch sheet of paper is called "letter size". an 8.5 by 14 inch sheet of paper is called "legal size". Show your calculations and name the paper size that is closest to a golden rectangle.

REMEMBER

The golden ration is an irrational number. It is equal to $\dfrac{(\sqrt{5}+1)}{2} = 1.61803\ldots$

Example 2:

A Number	B Col A + 1	C Recip Col B	D Col C + 1	E Recip Col D	F Col E + 1	G Recip Col F
(N)	(N + 1)	$\dfrac{1}{(N+1)}$	$\dfrac{1}{(N+1)} + 1$	$\dfrac{N+1}{(N+2)}$	$\dfrac{2N+3}{N+2}$	$\dfrac{N+2}{2N+3}$
4	5	0.2	1.2	$0.\overline{833}$	$1.\overline{833}$	$0.\overline{5454}$

Solution 2:

Using the TI-83 Plus graphing calculator.

4 + 1	Press **4** key, Press **+** key, Press **1** key
5	Press **ENTER** key
Ans^{-1}	Press **x^{-1}** reciprocal key
.2	Press **ENTER** key
Ans + 1	Press **+** key, Press **1** key
1.2	Press **ENTER** key
Ans^{-1}	Press **x^{-1}** reciprocal key
.8333333333	Press **ENTER** key
Ans + 1	Press **+** key, Press **1** key
1.833333333	Press **ENTER** key

Continuing with this procedure, we get the additional values:

.5454545455	1.545454545	.6470588235	1.6470588235
.6071428571	1.607142857	.6222222222	1.622222222
.6164383562	1.616438356	.6186440678	1.618644068
.6178010471	1.617801047	.6181229773	1.618122977
.618	1.618	.6180469716	1.618046972
.6180290298	1.61802903	.6180358829	1.618035883
.6180332652	1.618033265	.6180342651	1.618034265

[These values eventually differ by exactly 1]   [The golden ratio becomes 1.61803...]

4. Today's analog TV's have an aspect ratio of 4:3. The new HDTV digital TV's with a wide screen format have an aspect ratio of 16:9. Calculate the decimal value of the aspect ratio of the analog and digital TV's. Explain which type TV screen is almost a golden rectangle.

REMEMBER

Using the quadratic formula with the TI-83+ graphing calculator to solve a quadratic equation.

Example 1: Find the roots of the equation $2x^2 - 5x + 1 = 0$

Solution: Enter the coefficients 2, - 5, and 1 by pressing the following keys:

Press		2		STO→	ALPHA	A		ALPHA	:
		(–)	5		STO→	ALPHA	B	ALPHA	:
		1		STO→	ALPHA	C			

Now store the values to the variables A, B, and C:

Press   **ENTER**

Enter the expression for one of the solutions for the quadratic formula,

$(- B + \sqrt{(B^2 - 4AC)}) \div (2A)$

Press	(	(–)	ALPHA	B	+	2nd	√	ALPHA	B	x²
	–	4	ALPHA	A	ALPHA	C	)	)		
	÷ (	2	ALPHA	A	)					

Press   **ENTER** to find one solution is 2.280776406

This is seen on the screen:

```
2→A: -5→B: 1→C
                    1
(-B+√ (B²-4AC)) / (
2A)
          2.280776406
```

To save keystrokes, recall the last expression you entered, and then edit it for the negative radical calculation.

Press	**2nd**	**ENTRY**	This recalls fraction conversion entry.
Press	**2nd**	**ENTRY**	This recalls the quadratic formula.
Press	↑		to move cursor onto the + sign in the formula.
Press	–		to edit the quadratic formula for the negative radical value.
Press	**ENTER**		to find the other solution **0.2192235936**

REMEMBER

Using the quadratic formula with the TI-83+ graphing calculator to solve a quadratic equation.

Example 2: Find roots of the equation $2x^2 - 3x + 3 = 0$

Solution 2: When you set $a + bi$ complex number mode, the TI-83+

displays complex results.

Press **MODE**

Press $\downarrow$ 6 times and $\rightarrow$ once to position the cursor over $a + bi$.

Press **ENTER** to select $a + bi$ complex number mode.

Press **2nd** **QUIT** to return to the home screen.

Press **CLEAR** to clear the home screen.

Enter the coefficients 2, – 3, and 3 by pressing the following keys:

Press 2 STO→ ALPHA A ALPHA :

  (–) 3 STO→ ALPHA B ALPHA :

  3 STO→ ALPHA C

Now store the values to the variables A, B, and C:

Press **ENTER**

Enter the expression for one of the solutions for the quadratic formula,

$(- B + \sqrt{(B^2 - 4AC)}) \div (2A)$

Press ((–) ALPHA B + 2nd $\sqrt{}$ ALPHA B x^2

  – 4 ALPHA A ALPHA C))

  ÷ (2 ALPHA A)

Press **ENTER** to find one solution is $.75 + .9682458366i$

This is seen on the screen:

```
2→A: -3→B: 3→C
                    3
(-B+√ (B²-4AC)) / (
2A)
.75 + .9682458366i
```

Follow the last 5 step procedure on the prior page. The other solution is **.75 - .9682458366i**

Note that the two roots are complex conjugates.

REMEMBER

Discriminant and Nature of the roots of a quadratic equation.

For the quadratic equation $Ax^2 + Bx + C = 0$, the discriminant is $B^2 - 4AC$ [$A \neq 0$]

Value of discriminant [$B^2 - 4AC$]	Nature of the roots [intersection with x-axis]	Sketch of the parabola [$A > 0$] [$A < 0$]
$= 0$	Real, 2 equal, rational	
> 0 and a perfect square	Real, 2 *un*equal, rational	
> 0 and *not* a perfect square	Real, 2 *un*equal, *ir*rational	
< 0	Imaginary complex conjugates	

Sum of the roots: $r_1 + r_2 = -\dfrac{B}{A}$ Product of the roots: $r_1 \cdot r_2 = \dfrac{C}{A}$

$Ax^2 + Bx + C = 0$ [quadratic equation]

$\dfrac{Ax^2}{A} + \dfrac{Bx}{A} + \dfrac{C}{A} = \dfrac{0}{A}$ [divide by A]

$x^2 - [$ Sum of the roots $]\ x + $ Product of the roots $= 0$ [substitute sum & product]

Example: Find the quadratic equation whose sum of the roots $= 4$ and whose product of the roots $= -3$.

Solution: $x^2 - 4x - 3 = 0$

UNIT 2
NUMBER AND NUMERATION

Apply rational and irrational numbers (continued)

Example:

The altitude of a fired projectile as a function of time can be given as $h = -16t^2 + v_u t + h_o$ where v_u is the upward component of its initial velocity in feet per second and h_o is the altitude in feet from which it is fired.

A rocket is launched from a hilltop h_o feet above the desert with an initial upward velocity of v_u feet per second as shown in the figure below. When will it land on the desert?

a Discuss what the discriminant can tell you about the solution to this problem. (let $v_u = 400$ ft/sec and $h_o = 2400$ ft)

b Use the quadratic equation to find the solution.

c Explain your answer.

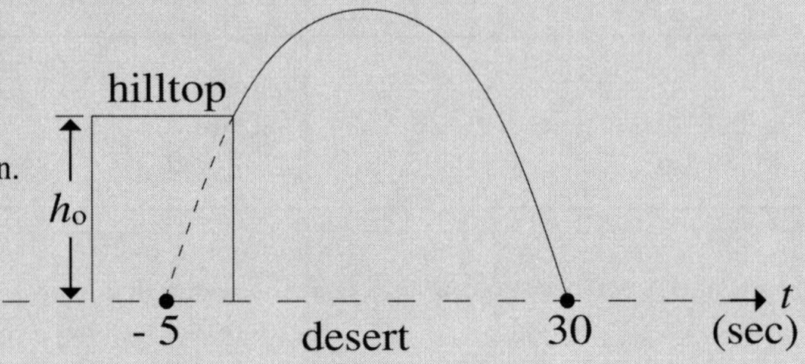

Solution:

a $h = -16t^2 + v_u t + h_o$

$0 = -16t^2 + 400t + 2400$ [The altitude, *h*, is 0 when the projectile lands.]

$0 = t^2 - 25t - 150$ [Simplify by dividing by – 16.]

Discrimination = $B^2 - 4AC = (-25)^2 - 4(1)(-150) = 625 + 600 = 1225$

1225 > 0 and a perfect square. Therefore the roots are Real, unequal; and rational.

b Using the quadratic equation and the TI-83 + graphing calculator as previously explained, the roots are – 5 and 30. We reject the – 5 root as can be seen on the graph above.

c The rocket will land in the desert 30 seconds after it is launched from the hilltop. When $h = 0$, the parabola crosses the *x*-axis which is, in this example, the desert.

1. Repeat the example above when $v_u = 320$ ft/sec and $h_o = 1280$ ft above the desert.

Apply rational and irrational numbers (continued)

2. An object moves along a line in such a way that its distance S in feet from a fixed point on the line at the end of t seconds is given by the equation $S = t^2 - 6t + 14$.

   Find the velocity of the object in feet per second when t = 8 seconds.

   a   using the formulas for the axis of symmetry $t_x = \dfrac{-B}{2A}$ and velocity, $v = \dfrac{S}{t_x}$

   b   using the 1st derivative of S respect to t, $\dfrac{dS}{dt}$

3. For what value k will the graph of $y = 3x^2 + 2x + k$ be tangent to the x-axis?

   Hint: The discriminant = 0 when the graph is tangent to the x-axis?

4. Find the positive value of B such that the graph of $y = x^2 + Bx + 9$ touches the x-axis in one and only one point. Show and explain your work.

5. Given : $(x + 3)(x - 1) = 5(x - 1)$, find:

   a   the roots of the equation

   b   the axis of symmetry

   c   the discriminant

Apply rational and irrational numbers (continued)

REMEMBER

Example: Refer to the example in the prior REMEMBER statement.

Given: $h = -16t^2 + 400t + 2400$

a   Discuss what the formula for the axis of symmetry can tell you about the problem and explain how to find the time it takes for the rocket to reach its maximum height.

b   Explain how to find the maximum height reached by the rocket.

Solution:

a   axis of symmetry $= \dfrac{-B}{2A} = \dfrac{-(400)}{2(-16)} = 12.5$ [t = 12.5 sec to reach max height]

[The axis of symmetry passes through the vertex or turning point. Since A < 0, a maximum.]

b $h = -16t^2 + 400t + 2400$

$h = -16(12.5)^2 + 400(12.5) + 2400$

$h = -2500 + 5000 + 2400$

$h = 4900$ ft   [Substitute the value of t]

An <u>alternate solution</u> is to start with the function: $h = -16t^2 + 400t + 2400$

Take the 1st derivative of h respect to t: $\dfrac{dh}{dt} = -32t + 400$

Since $\dfrac{dh}{dt}$ is the velocity and the velocity = 0 at the turning point, in this case the maximum,

we set $\dfrac{dh}{dt} = 0$ $0 = -32t + 400$

$32t = 400$

$t = 12.5$ sec

To find the height of the rocket when $t = 12.5$ sec, substitute the value of t as shown in part b.

1.   Repeat the example above for $h = -16t^2 + 320t + 1280$

REMEMBER

Example:

A rocket is launched to intercept a high flying jet.
The rocket follows the path of a parabola according
to the function: $h = -16t^2 + v_u t + h_0$ where
h is the altitude in feet after t seconds,
v_u is the upward component of its initial velocity in ft/sec,
h_0 is the altitude in feet from which it is fired.

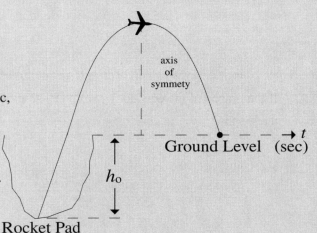

The rocket is launched from a pad that is 20 feet below
the ground level. Its initial upward velocity is 500 ft/sec.
The rocket intercepts the jet.

Using the equation for the axis of symmetry,
a   find the time it takes for the rocket to intercept the jet.
b   find the maximum height of the jet when intercepted.
    Explain and show how your conclusion was made.

Solution:
a $h = -16t^2 + v_u t + h_0$ [given that the distance, h, is a function of time, t.]
     $h = -16t^2 + 500t + (-20)$ [-20 since the pad is 20 ft *below* ground level]
     $h = -16t^2 + 500t - 20$ [A $= -16$, B $= 500$, C $= -20$]

     axis of symmetry, $t = \dfrac{-B}{2A}$ $= \dfrac{-500}{2(-16)}$ $= \dfrac{-500}{-32}$ $= 15.625$ seconds

b $h = -16t^2 + 500t - 20$
     $h = -16(15.625)^2 + 500(15.625) - 20$
     $h = -3906.25 + 7812.5 - 20$
     $h = -3886.25$ feet

The maximum height that the rocket can travel is 3886.25 ft.
Therefore the jet to be intercepted can be flying no higher than 3886.25 ft.

UNIT 2
NUMBER AND NUMERATION

Apply rational and irrational numbers (continued)

1. If the equation of the axis of symmetry of $2x^2 - px + 7 = 0$ is $x = 3$, find the value of p.

2. If the graphs of the equations $y = x^2 - x - 2$ and $y = 2x^2 - 2x - 4$ are drawn on the same set of axes, the graphs

   (1) coincide   (3) have the same y-intercepts

   (2) have the same x-intercepts   (4) do not intersect

3. If a jet is flying at a height of 5280 ft above ground level, and the rocket is fired from ground level with an initial upward velocity, v_u, of 592 ft/sec, find the time, t, in seconds it takes for the rocket to intercept the jet. Explain how many values of t you found.

$[\, h = -16t^2 + v_u t + h_0 \,]$ h is the altitude in feet of a projectile t seconds after firing.

                                      h_0 is the altitude in feet from which it was fired.

For additional practice problems on Quadratics, refer to the Westsea Publishing
SEQUENTIAL MATHEMATICS 3 Regents Exam Review Workbook
pages 27 to 31, and 107 to 108.

UNIT 2
NUMBER AND NUMERATION

Graphing a Parabola

Example:

a. Draw the graph of the equation
   $y = x^2 - 4x - 3$ for all values
   of x between $-1 \leq x \leq 5$.

b. What is the equation of the axis
   of symmetry?

c. What are the coordinates of the
   turning point?

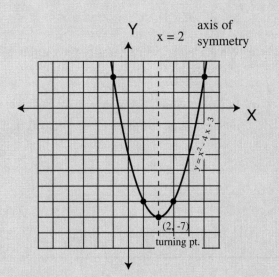

Y x = 2 axis of symmetry

(2, -7) turning pt.

x	$x^2 - 4x - 3$	y
-1	$(-1)^2 - 4(-1) - 3$ $1 + 4 - 3$	2
0	$0^2 - 4(0) - 3$ $0 - 0 - 3$	-3
1	$1^2 - 4(1) - 3$ $1 - 4 - 3$	-6
2	$2^2 - 4(2) - 3$ $4 - 8 - 3$	-7
3	$3^2 - 4(3) - 3$ $9 - 12 - 3$	-6
4	$4^2 - 4(4) - 3$ $16 - 16 - 3$	-3
5	$5^2 - 4(5) - 3$ $25 - 20 - 3$	2

b. $x = \dfrac{-b}{2a}$

$x = \dfrac{-(-4)}{2(1)} = \dfrac{4}{2}$

x = 2 is the
axis of symmetry

c. To get the turning
   pt. put the x value
   for the axis of
   symmetry into
   the equation

$y = x^2 - 4x - 3$

$y = (2)^2 - 4(2) - 3$

$y = 4 - 8 - 3$

$y = 7$

Therefore the turning point
is (2, -7).

1. a. Draw the graph of the equation $y = x^2 + 4x - 5$
   for all values of x such that $-5 \leq x \leq 1$.

   b. What are the coordinates of the turning point
      of $y = x^2 + 4x - 5$?

   c. What are the roots of $x^2 + 4x - 5 = 0$?

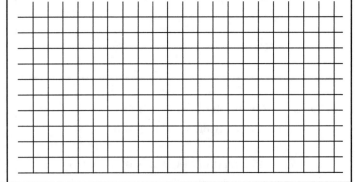

2. a. Find, in radical form, the roots of
      $x^2 - 8x + 11 = 0$.

   b. Draw the graph of the equation
      $y = x^2 - 8x + 11$ including all values of x
      such that $1 \leq x \leq 7$.

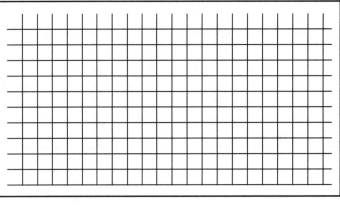

37

Graphing a Parabola (continued)

3. a. Draw the graph of the equation $y = x^2 - 2x - 2$
    for all values between $-2 \leq x \leq 4$.

    b. What are the coordinates of the turning point
    of the graph?

    c. Between which two consecutive positive
    integers does a root of $x^2 - 2x - 2 = 0$ lie?

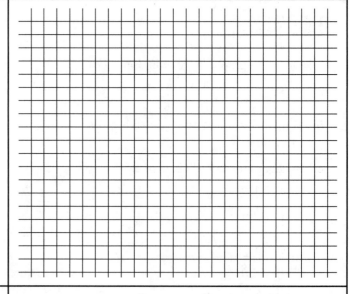

4. a. Find the roots of the equation $x^2 - 4x - 4 = 0$.
    [Answers may be left in radical form.]

    b. Draw the graph of the equation $y = x^2 - 4x - 4$,
    using all integral values of x such that
    $-1 \leq x \leq 5$.

    c. Based on the graph drawn in part "b," between
    which two positive consecutive integers does
    the value $y = 0$ lie?

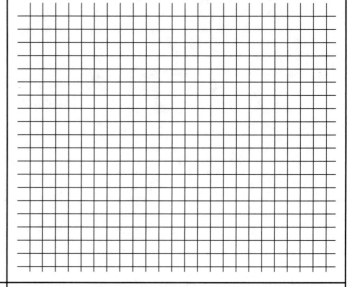

5. a. Draw the graph of the equation $y = -x^2 + 6x + 1$
    for all values from $x = 0$ to $x = 6$.

    b. Write an equation of the axis of symmetry of
    the graph drawn in part a.

    c. What are the coordinates of the turning point?

    d. Write an equation of a circle whose radius is 6
    and whose center is the y-intercept of the graph
    drawn in part a.

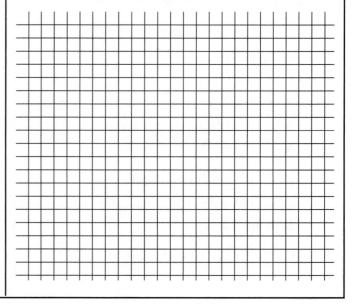

UNIT 2
NUMBER AND NUMERATION

Solving a system of equations, Graphically

To solve a system of equations graphically

1. Graph each equation on the same set of axis.
2. Locate the coordinates of the point or points of intersection.
3. Check your answers in both equations.

$y = x^2 - 2x + 3$

Example: a Draw the graph of the equation $y = x^2 - 2x + 3$ for all values of x such that $-2 \leq x \leq 4$.

     b On the same set of axis, draw the graph of the equation $y - x = 3$.

     c Using the graphs draw in parts a and b, determine the solution set of the system

$$y = x^2 - 2x + 3$$
$$y - x = 3$$

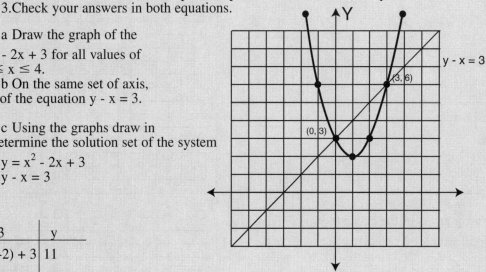

Solution:

x	$x^2 - 2x + 3$	y
-2	$(-2)^2 - 2(-2) + 3$ $4 + 4 + 3$	11
-1	$(-1)^2 - 2(-1) + 3$ $1 + 2 + 3$	6
0	$0 - 2(0) + 3$	3
1	$1^2 - 2(1) + 3$ $1 - 2 + 3$	2
2	$2^2 - 2(2) + 3$ $4 - 4 + 3$	3
3	$3^2 - 2(3) + 3$ $9 - 6 + 3$	6
4	$4^2 - 2(4) + 3$ $16 - 8 + 3$	11

Graph: $y - x = 3$
           $y = x + 3$
           slope = 1
           y - intercept = 3

check: (0, 3)

$y = x^2 - 2x + 3$ $y - x = 3$

$3 = 0^2 - 2(0) + 3$ $3 - 0 = 3$
$3 = 3$ $3 = 3$

check: (3, 6)

$y = x^2 - 2x + 3$ $y - x = 3$

$6 = 3^2 - 2(3) + 3$ $6 - 3 = 3$
$6 = 9 - 6 + 3$ $3 = 3$
$6 = 6$

The solutions are (0, 3) and (3, 6)

---

1. a   Draw the graph of the equation
     $y = 2x^2 + 3x - 1$ for all values
     of x such that $-3 \leq x \leq 2$.

   b   On the same set of axis, draw the graph of
     the equation $y = 2x$.

   c   Using the graphs draw in parts a and b,
     determine the solution set of the system

$$y = 2x^2 + 3x - 1$$
$$y = 2x$$

   d   Check your answer

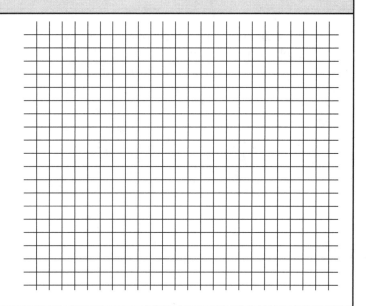

UNIT 2
NUMBER AND NUMERATION

2. Solve the following system of equations graphically and check.

   $y = -x^2 - 4x + 1$

   $y + 4x = -3$

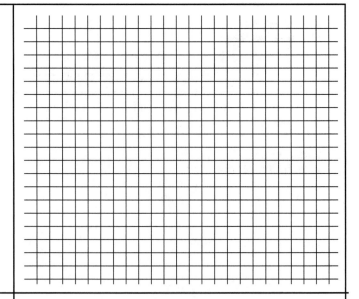

3. a Draw a graph of the equation $y = -x^2 + 6x - 3$ for all values of x such that $0 \leq x \leq 6$.

   b On the same set of axes draw the graph of $y = 3x - 1$.

   c Using the graphs draw in parts a and b, determine the solution of the system
   $y = -x^2 + 6x - 3$
   $y = 3x - 1$

   d Check your answers.

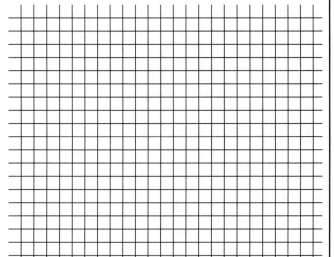

4. Solve the following system of equations graphically and check:

   $y = \dfrac{x^2}{2} - 2x$

   $y - 2x = -6$

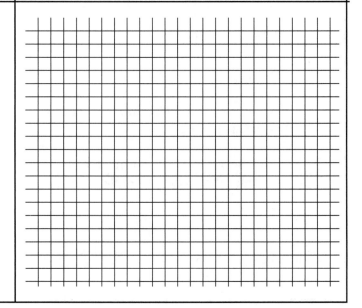

UNIT 2
NUMBER AND NUMERATION

Solving a system of equations, Algebraically

1. Solve the linear equation for either x or y.
2. Substitute the x or y into the quadratic equation.
3. Solve the new quadratic equation.
4. Substitute the two solutions in the linear equation.
5. Check both ordered pairs.

Example:

Solve the following system of equations and check:

$y - 3x = -5$

$y = x^2 - 5x + 10$ Step 1

Solution: $y - 3x = -5$

           $y = 3x - 5$ Step 2

           $y = x^2 - 5x + 10$

       $3x - 5 = x^2 - 5x + 10$ Step 3

           $0 = x^2 - 8x + 15$

           $0 = (x - 5)\ (x - 3)$

    $x - 5 = 0$ $x - 3 = 0$

       $x = 5$ $x = 3$

      $y = 3x - 5$ $y = 3x - 5$

      $y = 3(5) - 5$ $y = 3(3) - 5$

      $y = 15 - 5 = 10$ $y = 9 - 5 = 4$

Check: (5, 10)	(3, 4)
$10 - 3(5) = -5$	$4 - 3(3) = -5$
$10 - 15 = -5$	$4 - 9 = -5$
$-5 = -5$	$-5 = -5$
$10 = 5 - 5(5) + 10$	$4 = 9 - 15 + 10$
$10 = 2 - 25 + 10$	$4 = 9 - 15 + 10$
$10 = 10$	$4 = 4$

Therefore, solution is (5, 10) and (3, 4)

---

1. Solve the following system of equations algebraically and check.

    $y + 3x = 6$

    $y + x^2 - 2x - 6$

---

2. Solve the following system of equations algebraically and check.

    $y = x^2 - 5$

    $y = 3x - 1$

---

3. Solve the following system of equations algebraically and check.

    $y = x^2 + x + 3$

    $y + x = 6$

Solving a system of equations, Algebraically (continued)

4. Solve the following system of equations algebraically and check.

$y = x^2 + 5x + 2$

$y = 3x + 5$

5. Solve the following system of equations algebraically and check.

$x^2 + y^2 = 32$

$y - x = 0$

6. Solve the following system of equations algebraically and check.

$y = 3x + 12$

$y = x^2 + 2x - 18$

7. Solve the following system of equations algebraically and check.

$y = x^2 + 7x + 22$

$y + 3x = 1$

8. Solve the following system of equations algebraically and check.

$x^2 + y^2 = 41$

$y - x = -1$

UNIT 2
NUMBER AND NUMERATION

Introduction to Complex Numbers

REMEMBER

A complex number can be written in the form $a + bi$ where the real part is represented by a and the imaginary part is represented by bi.

The absolute value of a complex number, $|a + bi| = \sqrt{a^2 + b^2}$

The absolute value of a complex number, $|a - bi| = \sqrt{a^2 + b^2}$

The complex conjugate of $a + bi$ is $a - bi$. The complex conjugate of $a - bi$ is $a + bi$.

The additive inverse of $a + bi$ is $-(a + bi)$ or $-a - bi$.

The multiplicative inverse of $a + bi$ is $\dfrac{1}{a + bi}$ where the denominator must be rationalized.

$$\frac{1}{a + bi} = \frac{1(a - bi)}{(a + bi)(a - bi)} = \frac{a - bi}{a^2 - abi + abi - i^2} = \frac{a - bi}{a^2 - i^2} = \frac{a - bi}{a^2 + 1}$$

[*multiplying by the conjugate*]   [*F.O.I.L*]   [$-i^2 = 1$]

The distributive property of multiplication for a complex number: $n(a + bi) = na + nbi$

If two complex numbers are equal, $a + bi = r + wi$, then $a = r$ and $b = w$.

Complex numbers may be added, subtracted, multiplied and divided.

Addition: $(a + bi) + (r + wi) = (a + r) + (b + w)i$

Subtraction: $(a + bi) - (r + wi) = (a - r) + (b - w)i$

Multiplication: $(a + bi)(a - bi) = a^2 - abi + abi - b^2i^2 = a^2 - b^2i^2 = a^2 + b^2$

Multiplication: $(a + bi)(r + wi) = ar + awi + bri + bwi^2 = ar + awi + bri - bw$

$$= (ar - bw) + (aw + br)i$$

Division: $\dfrac{(a + bi)}{(r + wi)} = \dfrac{(a + bi)}{(r + wi)} \cdot \dfrac{(r - wi)}{(r - wi)} = \dfrac{ar - awi + bri - bwi^2}{r^2 - rwi + rwi - w^2i^2 - w^2i^2} = \dfrac{(ar + bw) - (aw - br)i}{r^2 + w^2}$

43

UNIT 3
NUMBER AND NUMERATION

Use addition, subtraction, multiplication, division, and exponentiation of fractions

Addition and Subtraction of Fractions

REMEMBER

To add or subtract algebraic fractions, first find the least common denominator and then combine the numerators.

Example: Add the fractions $\dfrac{3}{x+4} + \dfrac{2}{x}$

Solution:

1. Find the LCD

$$\dfrac{3}{x+4} + \dfrac{2}{x} = \dfrac{3x}{x(x+4)} + \dfrac{2(x+4)}{x(x+4)}$$

2. Simplify:

$$= \dfrac{3x+2x+8}{x(x+4)}$$

$$= \dfrac{5x+8}{x^2+4x} \quad \text{ans.}$$

Multiplication and Division of Fractions

REMEMBER

To multiply and divide fractions, do all factoring *before* any simplifications.

Example: For all values of x for which it is defined, simplify:

$$\dfrac{5x^2-5x-60}{4x^2-x} \cdot \dfrac{x-3x-10}{x-4} \cdot \dfrac{8x-2x}{x^2-2x-15}$$

Solution: $\dfrac{5(x^2-x-12)}{x(4x-1)} \cdot \dfrac{(x+2)(x-5)}{x-4} \cdot \dfrac{2x(4x-1)}{(x+3)(x-5)}$

$$\dfrac{5(x+3)(x-4)}{x(4x-1)} \cdot \dfrac{(x+2)(x-5)}{x-4} \cdot \dfrac{2x(4x-1)}{(x+3)(x-5)}$$

$$5 \quad \cdot \quad (x+2) \quad \cdot \quad 2 \quad = \quad 10(x+2) \quad \text{ans.}$$

Exponentiation of Fractions

REMEMBER

Example: Find the value of $5x^0 + \left(\dfrac{6}{x}\right)^{-2}$ when $x = 6$.

Solution: Since $x^0 = 1$ and $\left(\dfrac{6}{x}\right)^{-2} = \left(\dfrac{x}{6}\right)^2 = \dfrac{x^2}{36}$ substitute into the original problem.

$$5x^0 + \left(\dfrac{6}{x}\right)^{-2} = 5(1) + \dfrac{x^2}{36} = 5 + \dfrac{6^2}{36} = 5 + 1 = 6 \quad \text{ans.}$$

UNIT 3
NUMBER AND NUMERATION

Use addition, subtraction, multiplication, division, and exponentiation of fractions (continued)

Example 1: $x = -\sqrt{9^2}$ Solution 1: $x = -\sqrt{81}$ $x = -9$

Example 2: $|x| = \sqrt{9^2}$ Solution 2: $|x| = \sqrt{81}$ $x = 9$

Example 3: $|x| = \sqrt{(-9)^2}$ Solution 3: $|x| = \sqrt{81}$ $x = 9$

Example 4: $|x| = \sqrt{-(9)^2}$ Solution 4: $|x| = \sqrt{-81}$ $|x| = i\sqrt{81}$ $x = 9i$

Example 5: $|x| = \sqrt[4]{81}$ Solution 5: $|x| = (81)^{\frac{1}{4}}$ $|x| = 3$

Example 6: $|x| = \sqrt[4]{(81)^2}$ Solution 6: $|x| = ((81)^2)^{\frac{1}{4}} = 81^{\frac{1}{2}} = 9$

Example 7: $\log_3 x^2 = 4$ Solution 7: $x^2 = 3^4$ $x^2 = 81$ $x = \pm 9$

Example 8: $\log_3 x^4 = 4$ Solution 8: $x^4 = 3^4$ $x = 3$

Example 9: $\log_2 \dfrac{(x^2 - 81)}{x - 9} = 4$ Solution 9: $\log_2 (x + 9) = 4$ $[\, x \neq 9\,]$ $2^4 = x + 9$ $x = 7$

Example 1:

Solve the equation $x^{\frac{3}{2}} = 64$
for the real value of x

Solution 1:

$$x^{\frac{3}{2}} = 64$$
$$\left(x^{\frac{3}{2}}\right)^{\frac{2}{3}} = (64)^{\frac{2}{3}}$$
$$x = (64)^{\frac{1}{3} \cdot 2}$$
$$x = 4^2$$
$$x = 16$$

Example 2:

Solve the equation $4^{(2x-3)} = \dfrac{1}{16}$ for x.

Solution 2:

$$4^{(2x-3)} = \frac{1}{16}$$
$$4^{(2x-3)} = 4^{-2}$$
$$2x - 3 = -2 \quad [\text{set exp} =\,]$$
$$2x = 3 - 2$$
$$x = 0.5$$

45

UNIT 3
NUMBER AND NUMERATION

Use addition, subtraction, multiplication, division, and exponentiation of fractions (continued)

1. Find the value of $3(x + 5)^0 + \sqrt[3]{x^4} - \left(\frac{4}{x}\right)^{-1}$ when $x = 8$

2. Find the value of $4x^0 + \left(\frac{3}{x}\right)^{-2} + \sqrt[3]{x^3}$ if $x = 3$

3. Solve for the real value of x: $x^{\frac{3}{2}} = \frac{1}{64}$

4. Solve for the real value of x: $27^{(2x + 4)} = 9^{(4x + 1)}$

5. Find the real root of the equation: $x^{\frac{3}{2}} = \frac{64}{125}$

6. Given: $y = \frac{x - 5}{x + 3}$ Solve for x in terms of y.

UNIT 3
NUMBER AND NUMERATION

Use addition, subtraction, multiplication, division, and exponentiation of fractions (continued)

7. If x is an integer > 0, which is the equivalent to $9x^{-\frac{1}{2}}$?

    (1) $3\sqrt{x}$ (3) $\dfrac{9}{x}$

    (2) $3x$ (4) $\dfrac{9\sqrt{x}}{x}$

8. If $y = 0$, which is the equivalent to $4y^{-2}$?

    (1) $\dfrac{1}{4}$ (3) $\dfrac{1}{16}$

    (2) undefined   (4) 4

9. If w is an integer > 0, which is the equivalent to $(27w)^{-\frac{1}{3}}$?

    (1) $\left(\dfrac{w}{3}\right)^{\frac{2}{3}}$ (3) $3\sqrt[3]{w}$

    (2) $\dfrac{27}{w^3}$ (4) none of these

10. Solve for t to the nearest integer.
$$2{,}400 = (5.4)^{0.584t}$$

Use addition, subtraction, multiplication, division, and exponentiation of fractions (continued)

---

11. Solve for y as a function of x:

$$x^2 = \frac{1 - y}{1 + y}$$

---

12. Combine into a single term:

$$\sqrt{-72} \; + \; \frac{3}{\sqrt{-8}}$$

---

13. If $f(x) = \dfrac{3x}{x^2 + 4}$ and $g(x) = \sqrt{x - 4}$

Find $(f \textbf{ o } g)(x)$ in simplified form.

---

14. Given the function:

$$h(x) = \frac{12 + x}{x}$$

Find the inverse function, $h^{-1}(x)$

For additional practice problems on fractions, refer to the Westsea Publishing
SEQUENTIAL MATHEMATICS 3 Regents Exam Review Workbook pages 2 to 10, and 79 to 84.

UNIT 3
NUMBER AND NUMERATION

Understanding and using the composition of functions and transformations

Translations

REMEMBER

A translation is a slide of x and/or y units.

For a translation $T_{r, s}$ $(x, y) \rightarrow (x + r, y + s)$

Example: What is the image of (-8, 1) after the transformation $T_{(2, -4)}$?

Solution: (-8 + 2, 1 - 4) = (-6, -3) ans.

Reflections

REMEMBER

Line Reflections (images that are mirrored over a line)		Examples	Solutions
(a) A reflection in the x-axis	$(x, y) \rightarrow (x, -y)$	(2, -4)	(2,4) ans.
(b) A reflection in the y-axis	$(x, y) \rightarrow (-x, y)$	(3, 5)	(-3,5) ans.
(c) A reflection in the line $y=x$	$(x, y) \rightarrow (y, x)$	(-1, 7)	(7,-1) ans.
(d) A reflection in the line $y=-x$	$(x, y) \rightarrow (-y, -x)$	(-6, 9)	(-9,6) ans.

Point Reflection in the Origin
$$(x, y) \rightarrow (-x, -y)$$

Example: What are the coordinates of the image of point P (-3, 2) when it is reflected in the origin?

Solution: P (-3, 2) $\rightarrow$ P^1 (3, -2) ans.

Rotations

REMEMBER

Rotations about the origin (ccw)		Examples	Solutions
(a) 90° ccw rotation	$(x, y) \rightarrow (-y, x)$	(-2, -4)	(4, -2) ans.
(b) 180° ccw rotation	$(x, y) \rightarrow (-x, -y)$	(-5, 3)	(5, -3) ans.
(c) 270° ccw rotation	$(x, y) \rightarrow (y, -x)$	(7, 1)	(1, -7) ans.
(d) 360° ccw rotation	$(x, y) \rightarrow (x, y)$	(-5, 8)	(-5, 8) ans.

NOTE: A 180° ccw rotation is equivalent to a Point Reflection in the Origin

Dilations

REMEMBER

A dilation is magnification or reduction of a figure.
For a dilation of D_n $(x,y) \rightarrow (nx,ny)$.

Example: Find the image of (5, -1) under the dilation D_3.

Solution: (5, – 1) $\rightarrow$ (15, – 3)   ans.

UNIT 3
OPERATIONS

Understanding and using the composition of functions and transformations (continued)

REMEMBER

Example: Point Q^1 is the image of point $Q(-3, 4)$ after a translation defined by $T_{(7, -1)}$.
Which other transformation on point Q would also produce Q^1?

(1) $r_{(y = \frac{-4}{3} x)}$ (3) $r_{(y = \frac{3}{4} x)}$

(2) $R_{90°}$ (4) $R_{270°}$

Solution: If $Q(-3, 4)$ is translated $T_{(7, -1)}$, its image is $Q^1(-3 + 7, 4 - 1) = Q^1(4, 3)$.

Plot both points Q and Q^1 on the coordinate axes.

Note the 3, 4, 5 rights triangles. If we call the origin point O, OQ and $OQ^1 = 5$ units

We can show $\triangle QOQ^1$ is a right triangle using the Pythagorean theorem or by showing

the slope of $\overline{OQ}$ is $\frac{-4}{3}$ and the slope of $\overline{OQ^1}$ is $\frac{3}{4}$ [$\overline{OQ} \perp \overline{OQ^1}$]

Since we translate from point Q to point Q^1, we are going 90° CW or –90°.
The coterminal angle to – 90° is 270°. Therefore the answer is $R_{270°}$ Answer (4)

---

1. If $Q(-3, 4)$ is reflected over the x axis, what would the coordinates of its image be?
   Explain or show your work.

---

2. If $Q(-3, 4)$ is reflected over the y axis, what would the coordinates of its image be?
   Explain or show your work.

---

3. Give the coterminal angles for the following degree measures.

a	30°	*f*	– 265°
b	– 45°	*g*	22.5°
c	90°	*h*	– 360°
d	– 180°	*i*	135°
e	265°	*j*	– 260.5°

UNIT 3
OPERATIONS

Understanding and using the composition of functions and transformations (continued)

Glide Reflection

REMEMBER

A glide reflection is a composition of a line reflection and a translation parallel to the line of reflection.

Example: Which composition of transformations represents a glide reflection of point A $(-1, 2)$?

(1) $r_{y-axis} \circ D_3 (A)$ 　　　　　(3) $r_{y=1} \circ r_{y=-x} (A)$

(2) $r_{x-axis} \circ R_{90°} (A)$ 　　　　(4) $T_{0,-5} \circ r_{y-axis} (A)$

Solution: $r_{y-axis} (-1, 2) \rightarrow (1, 2)$

$T_{0,-5} (1, 2) \rightarrow (1, -3)$

Since the slide is parallel to the y-axis, (4) ans.

Compositions of Transformations

REMEMBER

Compositions of transformations are NOT commutative.

Example: In the accompanying figure, a and b are symmetry lines for regular pentagon ABCDE. Find $r_a \circ r_b (D)$.

Solution: $r_b (D)$ has an image at point E. $r_a (E)$ has an image at point B.   B ans.

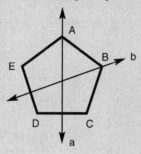

For practice problems on Transformations, refer to the Westsea Publishing

SEQUENTIAL MATHEMATICS 3 Regents Exam Review Workbook

pages 32 to 42, and 109 to 111.

Understanding and using the composition of functions and transformations (continued)

REMEMBER

$$y = Ax^2 + Bx + C$$

A	B	C	$y = Ax^2 + Bx + C$	Graphs as a function
> 0		y-intercept		Parabola vertex *maximum*
< 0		y-intercept		Parabola vertex *minimum*
= 0	Slope	y-intercept		Line

As A > 0 decreases, the parabola gets *wider* until A = 0 when the conic becomes a line.
As A < 0 becomes more negative, the parabola gets *narrower*.

Changing the value of B only, results in moving the coordinates of the *vertex*.
The width and y intercept remain the same.

Changing the value of C only, results in a translation, $T_{(0, y)}$

A	B	C	$y = Ax^2 + Bx + C$	Graphs as a function
≠ 0	≠ 0	≠ 0	$y = Ax^2 + Bx + C$	Parabola
≠ 0	≠ 0	= 0	$y = Ax^2 + Bx$	Parabola
≠ 0	= 0	≠ 0	$y = Ax^2 + C$	Parabola
≠ 0	= 0	= 0	$y = Ax^2$	Parabola
= 0	≠ 0	≠ 0	$y = Bx + C$	Diagonal line
= 0	= 0	≠ 0	$y = +C$	Horizontal line
= 0	≠ 0	= 0	$y = Bx$	Diagonal line
= 0	= 0	= 0	$y = 0$	Horizontal line

$$x = Ay^2 + By + C$$

A	B	C	$x = Ay^2 + By + C$	*Not* a function
> 0		x - intercept		Parabola vertex at *left*
< 0		x - intercept		Parabola vertex at *right*

axis of symmetry, $y = -\dfrac{B}{2A}$

Understanding and using the composition of functions and transformations (continued)

REMEMBER

If we keep A and C constant but *change* B, the <u>width and *y*-intercept</u> do *not* change.

equation	*axis of symmetry* = $\dfrac{-B}{2A}$	*turning point or vertex*	*roots*
$y_1 = x^2 + 2x + 0$	$x = -1$	$(-1, -1)$	$x = 0, x = -2$
$y_2 = x^2 + 4x + 0$	$x = -2$	$(-2, -4)$	$x = 0, x = -4$
$y_3 = x^2 + 6x + 0$	$x = -3$	$(-3, -9)$	$x = 0, x = -6$

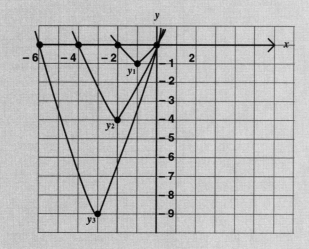

If we keep A and B constant but *change* C, we get a *translation* of $T_{(0, y)}$.

equation	*axis of symmetry* = $\dfrac{-B}{2A}$	*turning point or vertex*	*roots*
$y_1 = x^2 + 2x + 0$	$x = -1$	$(-1, -1)$	$x = 0, x = -2$
$y_2 = x^2 + 2x + 2$	$x = -1$	$(-1, 1)$	imaginary
$y_3 = x^2 + 2x + 4$	$x = -1$	$(-1, 3)$	imaginary

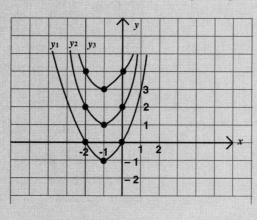

UNIT 3
OPERATIONS

Understanding and using the composition of functions and transformations (continued)

REMEMBER

If we let B = 0 and C = 1, but *change* A, we get a *parabola* with *changing width*.

As A gets *smaller*, the parabola *width* becomes *wider*.
When A = 0, the equation graphs as a line.
As A gets *more negative*, the *width* becomes *narrower*.

equation	vertex
$y_1 = 4x^2 + 1$	minimum
$y_2 = 2x^2 + 1$	minimum
$y_3 = 1x^2 + 1$	minimum
$y_4 = 0x^2 + 1$	*horizontal line*
$y_5 = -1x^2 + 1$	maximum
$y_6 = -2x^2 + 1$	maximum
$y_7 = -4x^2 + 1$	maximum

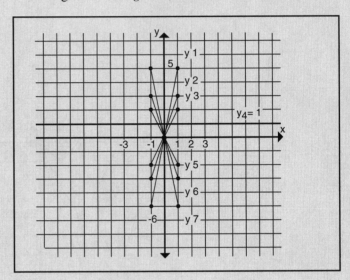

If we let B = 4 and C = 1, but *change* A, we get a *parabola* with *changing width*.

As A gets *smaller*, the parabola *width* becomes *wider*.
When A = 0, the equation graphs as a line.
As A gets *more negative*, the *width* becomes *narrower*.

equation	vertex
$y_1 = 4x^2 + 4x + 1$	minimum
$y_2 = 2x^2 + 4x + 1$	minimum
$y_3 = 1x^2 + 4x + 1$	minimum
$y_4 = 0x^2 + 4x + 1$	line
$y_5 = -1x^2 + 4x + 1$	maximum
$y_6 = -2x^2 + 4x + 1$	maximum
$y_7 = -4x^2 + 4x + 1$	maximum

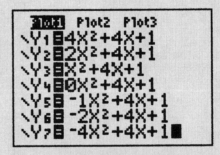

Press Y = key

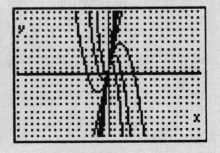

Press GRAPH key

54

UNIT 3
OPERATIONS

Understanding and using the composition of functions and transformations (continued)

REMEMBER

Graphs symmetric to the x and y-axes or the origin, $(0, 0)$.

CIRCLE:
$x^2 + y^2 = r^2$

Two concentric circles, center: $(0, 0)$
$x^2 + y^2 = 25$ where $r = 5$
$x^2 + y^2 = 81$ where $r = 9$

ELLIPSE:
$Ax^2 + By^2 = C$

$x^2 + 4y^2 = 36$

$\dfrac{x^2}{36} + \dfrac{4x^2}{36} = 1$

x - intercept: $(6, 0)$
y - intercept: $(0, 3)$ $A < B$

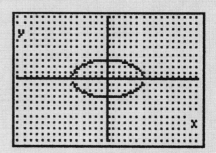

ELLIPSE:
$Ax^2 + By^2 = C$

$4x^2 + y^2 = 36$
$\dfrac{4x^2}{36} + \dfrac{y^2}{36} = 1$

x - intercept: $(3, 0)$
y - intercept: $(0, 6)$ $A > B$

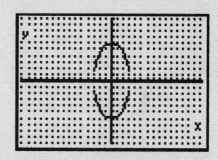

HYPERBOLA:
$Ax^2 - By^2 = C$

$x^2 - 4y^2 = 36$
$\dfrac{x^2}{36} - \dfrac{4y^2}{36} = 1$

x - intercept: $(6, 0)$
no y - intercept

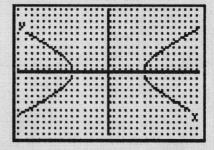

HYPERBOLA:
$Ay^2 - Bx^2 = C$

$4x^2 - y^2 = 36$
$\dfrac{4y^2}{36} - \dfrac{x^2}{36} = 1$

no x - intercept
y - intercept: $(0, 3)$

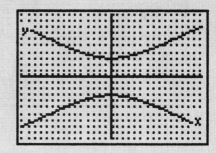

UNIT 3
OPERATIONS

Understanding and using the composition of functions and transformations (continued)

<u>Graphs symmetric to the *x* and *y*-axes or the origin, (0, 0).</u>
<u>Inverse Variation</u>

HYPERBOLA
$xy = 24$

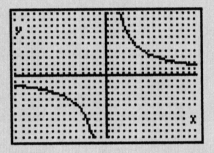

HYPERBOLA
$xy = -24$

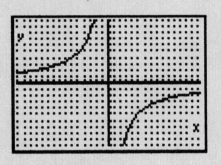

Quad I and III

Quad II and IV

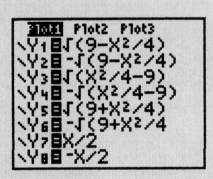

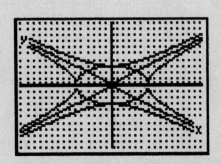

The equations of the parabola, hyperbolas, and asymptote lines at the left are illustrated at the bottom left by the graphing calculator and at the bottom right by a paper graph

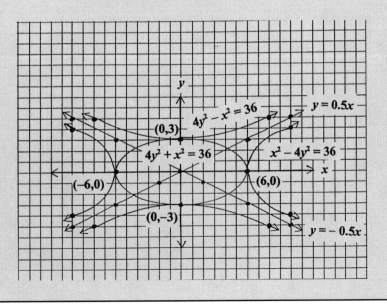

56

Understanding and using the composition of functions and transformations (continued)

1. Using the *graphing calculator*, complete the table.

Equation	Conic type	Plot 1	Sketch
$4x^2 + 4y^2 = 36$		$y_1 =$	
$4x^2 + y^2 = 36$		$y_2 =$	
$x^2 + 4y^2 = 36$		$y_3 =$	
$x^2 - y^2 = 36$		$y_4 =$	
$4x^2 - y^2 = 36$		$y_5 =$	
$x^2 - 4y^2 = 36$		$y_6 =$	
$xy = 36$		$y_7 =$	
$xy = -36$		$y_8 =$	
$y = 2x$		$y_9 =$	
$y = -2x$		$y_{10} =$	

UNIT 3
OPERATIONS

Understanding and using the composition of functions and transformations (continued)

2. Three cathedral windows are in the shape of parabolic arches. The equation of the middle arch can be expressed as $y = -2x^2 + 8$ with a range of $0 \leq y \leq 8$. The arch on the left is created by the transformation $T_{-6, 0}$ of the middle arch. The arch on the right is created by the reflection of the middle arch over the line $x = 3$.

a Graph the equations of the three arches and label them left, L, middle, M and right, R.

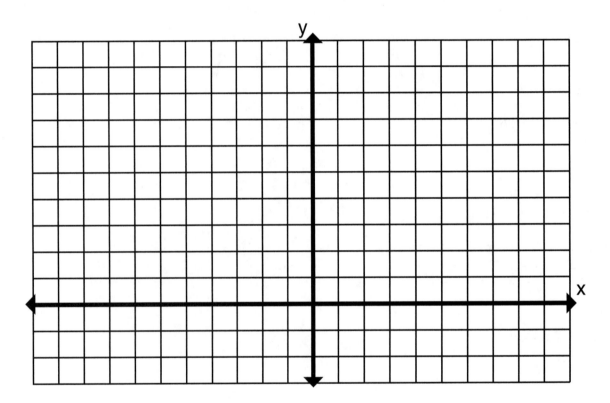

b Fill in the Table.

ARCH	EQUATION	ROOTS	MAXIMUM	AXIS OF SYMMETRY
M	$y = -2x^2 + 8$			$x = 0$
L		$\{-8, -4\}$		
R			$(6, 8)$	

UNIT 3
OPERATIONS

Understanding and using the composition of functions and transformations (continued)

REMEMBER

Isometry: A transformation that preserves distance.

Direct Isometry: A transformation the preserves distance and orientation.

Opposite Isometry: A transformation that preserves distance but changes orientation from clockwise to counterclockwise or <u>vice - versa.</u>

DIRECT ISOMETRY:

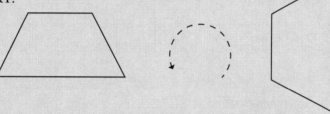

Congruent and
same orientation

OPPOSITE ISOMETRY:

Congruent but
rotated

<u>NOT</u> AN ISOMETRY:

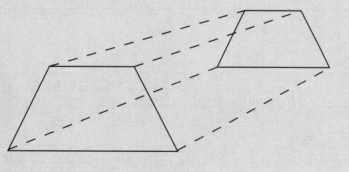

<u>not</u> Congruent

For practice problems on Isometries, refer to the Westsea Publishing

SEQUENTIAL MATHEMATICS 3 Regents Exam Review Workbook

pages 41 and 42.

UNIT 3
OPERATIONS

Domain of a Function

REMEMBER

The domain of a function is all values x for which f (x) exists.

A function is one to one if for each x in the domain there corresponds only one y in the range and for each y in the range there corresponds only one x in the domain.

Example: What is the domain of the function $f(x) = \sqrt{x - 3}$

Solution: $x - 3 \geq 0$
$x \geq 3$
Therefore $\{\, x \mid x \geq 3 \,\}$ ans.

Inverse of a Function

REMEMBER

To find the inverse of a function solve for the second variable in terms of the first variable and then interchange the variables.

If a function is one to one then its inverse is also a function

Example: What is the inverse of the function $y = \sqrt{x}$?

Solution: $x = y^2, y \geq 0$ solve for x in terms of y

$y = x^2$ interchange x and y

$y = x^2$ $x \geq 0$ ans.

Symmetry

REMEMBER

1. A figure has point symmetry if the figure is exactly the same when it is rotated 180° in either direction.
2. A figure has horizontal line symmetry if a horizontal line can be drawn through the middle so that half of it is mirrored on the other half.
3. A figure has vertical line symmetry if a vertical line can be drawn through the middle so that half of it is mirrored on the other half.

For additional practice problems, refer to the Westsea Publishing
SEQUENTIAL MATHEMATICS 3 Regents Exam Review Workbook
Domain of a Function: page 43
Inverse of a Function: page 44
Symmetry: page 40.

Understanding and using the composition of functions and transformations (continued)

REMEMBER

Example:

a   Draw f $(x) = 4x^2$ and f^{-1} (x) in the interval $0 \leq x \leq 1.5$ on the accompanying set of axes.
    Use increments of 0.25

b   State the coordinates of the points of intersection(s) of f (x) and f^{-1} (x).

Solution:

a

x	$4x^2$	f (x)	$(x, f(x))$	$(y, f^{-1}(x))$
0	$4(0)^2$	0	$(0, 0)$	$(0, 0)$
$\frac{1}{4}$	$4 \cdot \frac{1}{16}$	$\frac{1}{4}$	$(0.25, 0.25)$	$(0.25, 0.25)$
$\frac{1}{2}$	$4 \cdot \frac{1}{4}$	1	$(0.5, 1)$	$(1, 0.5)$
$\frac{3}{4}$	$4 \cdot \frac{9}{16}$	$\frac{9}{4}$	$(0.75, 2.25)$	$(2.25, 0.75)$
1	$4(1)^2$	4	$(1, 4)$	$(4, 1)$
$\frac{5}{4}$	$4 \cdot \frac{25}{16}$	$\frac{25}{4}$	$(1.25, 6.25)$	$(6.25, 1.25)$
$\frac{3}{2}$	$4 \cdot \frac{9}{4}$	9	$(1.5, 9)$	$(9, 1.5)$

b   The coordinates of the points of the intersection of f (x) and f^{-1} (x) are $(0, 0)$ and $(0.25, 0.25)$
    as see in the table above. The second point of intersection can also be found algebraically.

$$f(x) = 4x^2 \qquad f^{-1}(x) = 4y^2$$

$$y = 4x^2 \qquad x = 4y^2$$

$$y = 4(16y^4) \qquad \text{[substituting } 4y^2 \text{ for x]}$$

$$y = 64y^4 \qquad \text{[dividing when } y \textit{ not} \text{ equal to 0]}$$

$$y^3 = \frac{1}{64} \qquad y = \frac{1}{4} \qquad x = 4y^2 = 4 \cdot \frac{1}{16} \qquad x = \frac{1}{4} \qquad (0.25, 0.25)$$

UNIT 3
OPERATIONS

Understanding and using the composition of functions and transformations (continued)

a

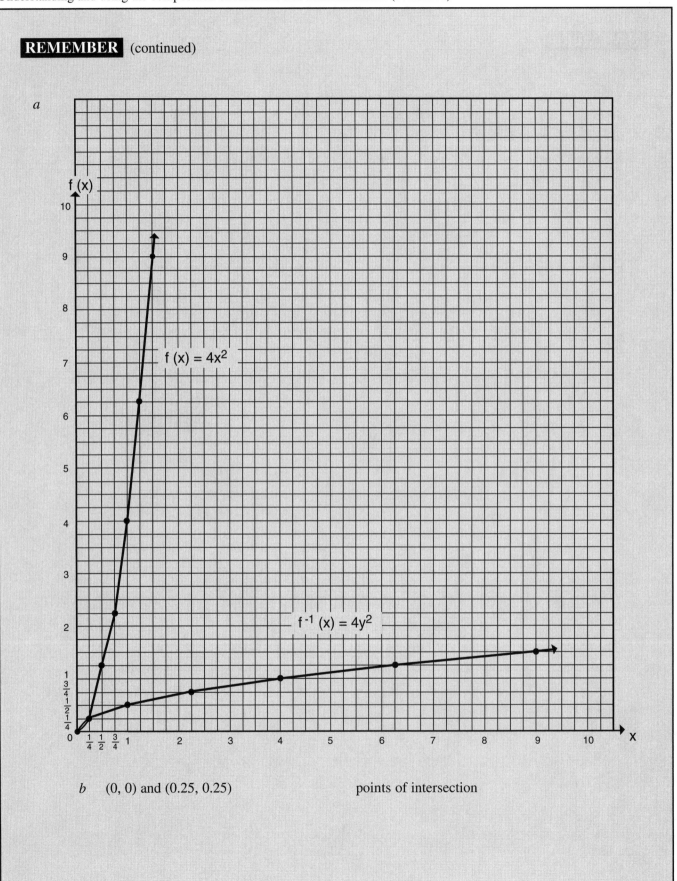

$f(x) = 4x^2$

$f^{-1}(x) = 4y^2$

b (0, 0) and (0.25, 0.25)   points of intersection

UNIT 3
OPERATIONS

Understanding and using the composition of functions and transformations (continued)

1. *a* Draw $f(x) = \dfrac{x^2}{2}$ and $f^{-1}(x)$ in the interval $0 \le x \le 4$ on the accompanying set of axes.

    b State the coordinates of the points of intersection(s) of $f(x)$ and $f^{-1}(x)$.

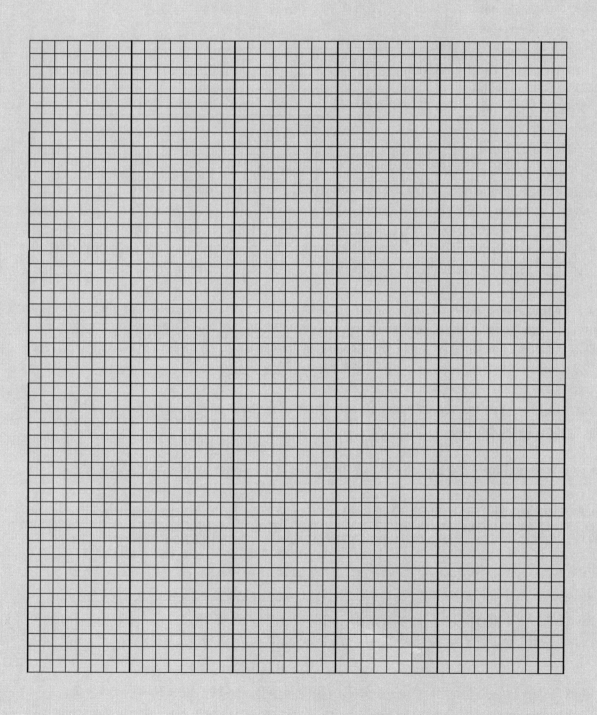

UNIT 3
OPERATIONS

Understanding and using the composition of functions and transformations (continued)

REMEMBER

1. <u>Relations and Functions:</u>   given the relation   y = 2x + 4
   - *a* State the **relation** if *x* is a positive integer < 4   Ans. { (1,6), (2, 8), (3, 10)}
   - *b* State the **domain**.   Ans. {1, 2, 3}
   - *c* State the **range**.   Ans. {6, 8, 10}

   d How did we find the **relation**?_____

   e How did we find the **domain**?_____

   f How did we find the **range**? _____

2. **A Relation is a Function:** if for any **one value of *x*,** you get only one value of ***y*.**
   State if the function is a relation:
   - *a* { (1, 2), (2, 3), (3, 4), (4, 5)} _____   *b* { (2, 1), (3, 2), (4, 3), (5, 4)} _____

   - *c* { (1, 2), (1, 3), (1, 4), (1, 5)} _____   *d* { (2, 1), (3, 1), (4, 1), (5, 1)} _____

3. **A Function is one to one:** if for each *x* in the domain there corresponds *only one y* in the range and
   for each *y* in the range there corresponds *only one x* in the domain.
   State if the examples in 2 above are one to one functions.
   - *a* _____   *b* _____   *c* _____   *d* _____

4. **Vertical Line Test:** If a vertical line **passes through more than one point** on any graph, the relation
   graphed is **not a function.**

5. Use a **Vertical line and a Horizontal line** to test any graph for <u>one to one correspondence</u>.

6. **Ordered Pair:** (*x*, *y*) or (*x*, f(*x*)) where f(*x*) is read as <u>"f of *x*"</u>. g(*x*), h(*x*) also used when more than one
   function is in the problem.

7. **Find f(2)**   if f(x) = 5x-3.   Solution: f(2) = 5(2) - 3 = 10 - 3 = 7.   f(2) = <u>7 Ans.</u>

   Find g(-1)   if g(x) = -6x + 2   Solution: g(-1) = -6(-1) + 2 = 6 + 2 = 8.   g(-1) = <u>8 Ans.</u>

   Find h(k)   if h(x) = x + 7   Solution: h(k) = <u>k + 7 Ans.</u>

   Find f(g(3)) if g(x) = 2x - 4 and f(x) = x + 1.   Solution: g(3) = 2(3) - 4 = 6 - 4 = 2.

                                           f(g(3)) = f(2) = 2 + 1 = <u>3 Ans.</u>

   Find 5f(2) + [4g(-1)][3h(k)]   Solution: 5f(2) = 5(7), 4g(-1) = 4(8), 3h(k) = 3(k + 7).

                                     35 + 32(3)(k + 7) = 35 + 96k + 672 = <u>707 + 96k Ans.</u>

UNIT 3
OPERATIONS

Understanding and using the composition of functions and transformations (continued)

Example: 1: If $f(x) = x^2 + 3x$, find $f(a - 1)$.

Solution 1: $f(x) = x^2 + 3x$

$f(a - 1) = (a - 1)^2 + 3(a - 1) = a^2 - 2a + 1 + 3a - 3 = a^2 + a - 2$ answer

Example 2: If $f(x) = (4x)^0 + x^{-\frac{2}{3}}$, find the value of $f(27)$.

Solution 2: $f(27) = 1 + 27^{-\frac{2}{3}} = 1 + \dfrac{1}{27^{\frac{2}{3}}} = 1 + \dfrac{1}{(27^{\frac{1}{3}})^2} = 1 + \dfrac{1}{3^2} = \dfrac{10}{9}$ ans.

---

1. If $g(a) = (a + 2)^2$, find $g(a + 1)$

---

2. If $f(x) = x^2 + 2x$, express $f(a - 2)$ as a product of a monomial and a binomial.

---

3. If $f(x) = kx^2$ and $f(2) = 12$, find k.

---

4. If $g(x) = \dfrac{1}{125^x}$, find $g\left(-\dfrac{1}{3}\right)$

Example: If $g(x) = 5x + 2$ and $h(x) = x^2$, find $(h \circ g)(3)$.

Solution: $g(3) = 5(3) + 2 = 15 + 2 = 17$

$(h \circ g)(3) = h(17) = (17)^2 = 289$ answer

---

1. If $f(x) = x - 3$ and $g(x) = x^2$, find the value of $(f \circ g)(2)$.

Hint: $(f \circ g(2) = f(g(2))$

UNIT 3
OPERATIONS

Understanding and using the composition of functions and transformations (continued)

REMEMBER

Example: If $f(x) = 2x^2 + 4$ and $g(x) = x - 3$, find the number that satisfies $f(x) = f \circ g(x)$.

Solution: $f(x) = 2x^2 + 4$

$f(x - 3) = 2(x - 3)^2 + 4 = 2(x^2 - 6x + 9) + 4 = 2x^2 - 12x + 22$

$(f \circ g)(x) = f(g(x)) = f(x - 3) = 2x^2 - 12x + 22$

For $f(x) = (f \circ g)(x)$

$2x^2 + 4 = 2x^2 - 12x + 22$

$4 = -12x + 22$

$12x = 18$

$x = 1.5$ answer

---

1. If $g(x) = 4x^2 + 2$ and $h(x) = x - 5$, which number satisfies $g(x) = (g \circ h)(x)$? Show all work

---

REMEMBER

Example 1: Find the inverse of the function $f(x) = 2x - 6$.

Solution 1: Let $f(x) = y$ then $y = 2x - 6$

Replace x with y and y with x so $x = 2y - 6$

Solve for y: $2y = x + 6$ $y = \dfrac{x + 6}{2}$ $y = \dfrac{x}{2} + 3$

Replace y with $f^{-1}(x)$ $f^{-1}(x) = \dfrac{x}{2} + 3$ answer

Example 2: Show whether $f(x)$ and $f^{-1}(x)$ in example 1 above are inverses of each other.

Solution 2: Functions are inverses of each other if : $f \circ g = g \circ f$

$f(x) = 2x - 6$ and $g(x) = f^{-1}(x) = \dfrac{x}{2} + 3$

$f \circ g = f(g(x))$ $g \circ f = g(f(x))$

$= f(\dfrac{x}{2} + 3)$ $= g(2x - 6)$

$= 2(\dfrac{x}{2} + 3) - 6$ $= \dfrac{1}{2}(2x - 6) + 3$

$= x + 6 - 6$ $= x - 3 + 3$

$f \circ g = x$ $g \circ f = x$

Since $f \circ g = g \circ f = x$, they *are inverse* of each other.   answer

---

UNIT 3
OPERATIONS

Understanding and using the composition of functions and transformations (continued)

1.   *a*   Find the point of intersection of $f(x) = 2x - 6$ and $f^{-1}(x) = 0.5x + 3$.

     b   Find the equation of the line containing the points (0, 0) and the point of intersection found in *a* above

     c   What conclusion can be made when functions and their inverses are graphed on the same set of coordinate axes?

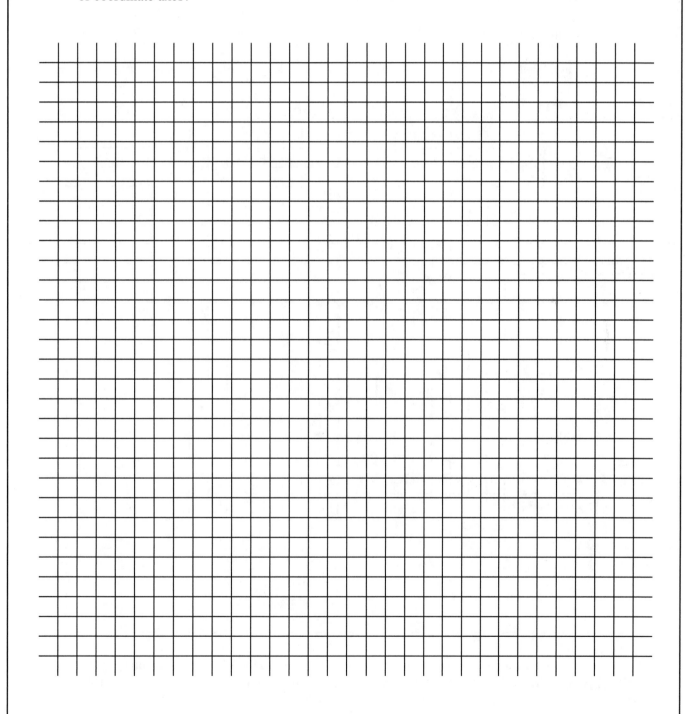

UNIT 3
OPERATIONS

Use transformations in the coordinate plane.

REMEMBER

Example: Given triangles ABC with coordinates A(-2, -3), B(0, -5) and C(5, -1).

a On graph paper, draw and label triangle ABC.

b Graph and label triangle A' B' C', the image of triangle ABC after translation $T_{(3, -4)}$.

c Graph and label triangle A" B" C", the image of triangle ABC after a reflection in the origin

d Graph and label triangle A''' B''' C''', the image of triangle ABC after a reflection in the line $y = x$.

Solution:

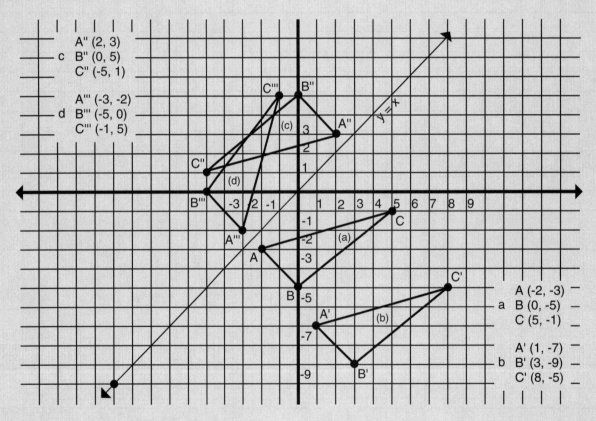

For additional problems on transformations, refer to the Westsea Publishing
SEQUENTIAL MATHEMATICS 3 Regents Exam Review Workbook pages 32 to 42, and 109 to 111.

UNIT 3
OPERATIONS

Use transformations in the coordinate plane (continued)

1. *a* Triangle ABC has coordinates a A(0, 6), B(-2, 0), and C(-4, 6).
On graph paper, draw and label △ ABC

   b Reflect the graph drawn in part *a* in the origin. Label the coordinates A', B', C'.

   c Dilate the graph drawn in part *b* using D$\frac{1}{2}$. Label the coordinates A", B", C".

   d Translate the graph drawn in part *c* using T$_{(3, 2)}$. Label the coordinates A''', B''', C'''.

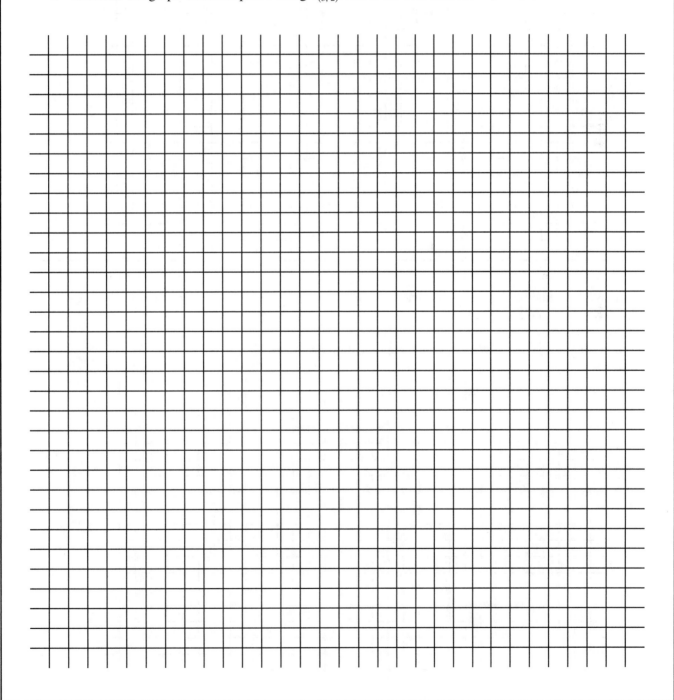

UNIT 3
OPERATIONS

Use transformations in the coordinate plane (continued)

2.   *a* Sketch the graph of $xy = -4$ from $x = -8$ to $x = 8$

      b On the same set of axes, reflect the graph drawn in part *a* in the *y* - axis and label it b.

      c Write an equation of the function graphed in part *b*.

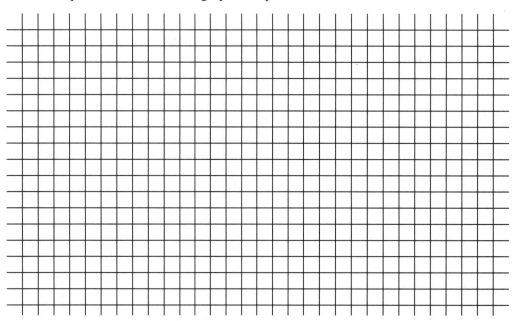

3.   *a* On the same set of axes, sketch and label the graphs of $y = \cos \frac{1}{2} x$ and $y = 2\sin x$ as x varies from 0 to 2π radians

      b Using the same set of axes, sketch the reflection of $y = \cos \frac{1}{2} x$ in the line $y = -2$

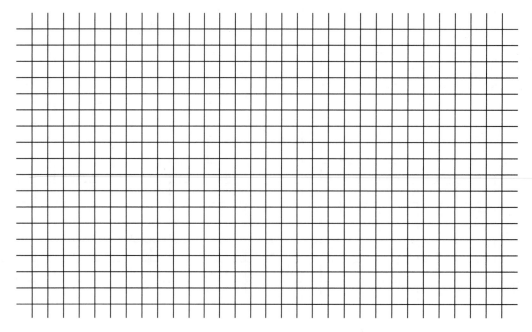

Complex numbers

REMEMBER

Real mode does *not* display complex results unless complex numbers are *entered as input*. The TI-83 Plus can display complex numbers in rectangular form (a + bi) and polor form (re^θi). Press **MODE** and press cursor keys to highlight **a + bi** form.

Adding complex numbers: (12 + 4i) + (-2 - 7i)
Press **CLEAR** press (Enter **12 + 4** press **2nd .)**
Press + press (press (-) key
Enter **2 - 7** press **2nd .)**
Press **ENTER** Answer shown is **10-3i**.

Subtracting complex numbers: (12 + 4i) - (-2 - 7i)
Press (Enter **12 + 4** press **2nd .)**
Press - press (press (-) key
Enter **2 - 7** press **2nd .)**
Press **ENTER** Answer shown is **14 + 11i**.

Multiplying complex numbers: (12 + 4i)(-2 - 7i)
Press (Enter **12 + 4** press **2nd .)**
Press × press (press (-) key
Enter **2 - 7** press **2nd .)**
Press **ENTER** Answer shown is **4 - 92i**.

Dividing complex numbers: $\dfrac{(6 + 2i)}{(3 + 4i)}$

method 1:
Press (Enter **6 + 2** press **2nd .)**
Press ÷ press (press (-) key
Enter **3 + 4** press **2nd .)**
Press **ENTER** Answer shown is **1.04 - .72i**
Press **MATH**   enter **1** to select Fraction
Press **ENTER** Answer shown is **26/25 - 18/25i**

method 2: Multiply the numerator and denominator by the complex conjugate of the denominator, (3 - 4i).

$$\frac{(6 + 2i)}{(3 + 4i)}\frac{(3 - 4i)}{(3 - 4i)} = \frac{18 - 24i + 6i - 8i^2}{9 - 12i + 12i - 16i^2} = \frac{18 - 18i + 8}{9 + 16} = \frac{26 - 18i}{25} = \frac{26}{25} - \frac{18}{25}i$$

Using the TI-83 Plus graphic calculator, we get an answer **1.04 - .72i**

Complex numbers (continued)

Addition, Subtraction, Multiplication, Division

REMEMBER

Example 1:   Simplify and express in a + bi form 3i (2 + 4i)

Solution 1:   3i (2) + 3i (4i)   = 6i - 12 = - 12 + 6i ans.

Example 2:   Find the sum of (9 + 2i) and (3 + 7i)

Solution 2:   Since (a + bi) + (c + di) = (a + c) + (b + d) i, the sum
can be found as (9 + 3) + (2 + 7) i = 12 + 9i ans.

Simplifying

REMEMBER

For any real numbers a and b where a and b > 0

$$\sqrt{-b^3} = \sqrt{-1}\sqrt{b^3} = i\sqrt{b^2}\sqrt{b} = ib\sqrt{b}$$

Examples:

$\sqrt{-8} = 2i\sqrt{2}$	$\sqrt{-12} = 2i\sqrt{3}$	$4\sqrt{-25} = 20i$
$2\sqrt{-32} = 8i\sqrt{2}$	$\dfrac{\sqrt{-75}}{\sqrt{-3}} = \dfrac{i\sqrt{75}}{i\sqrt{3}} =$	$\sqrt{25} = 5$

Conjugates, Multiplicative Inverse, Additive Inverse

REMEMBER

The conjugate of a + bi is a - bi. $(a + bi)(a - bi) = a^2 + b^2$

Example: Find the multiplicative inverse of 8 - 2i.

Solution: $\dfrac{1}{(8 - 2i)} \cdot \dfrac{(8 + 2i)}{(8 + 2i)} = \dfrac{8 + 2i}{64 + 4} = \dfrac{2}{17} + \dfrac{1}{34} i$ ans.

The additive inverse of a + bi is -(a + bi) = -a - bi

UNIT 3
OPERATIONS

Use rational exponents on real numbers and all operations on complex numbers

---

REMEMBER   Basic arithmetic operations with complex numbers

Example: What is the sum of $\sqrt{-2}$ and $\sqrt{-18}$?

      (1) $6i$ (3) $5i\sqrt{2}$

      (2) $2i\sqrt{5}$ (4) $4i\sqrt{2}$

Solution: $\sqrt{-2} + \sqrt{-18} = i\sqrt{2} + i\sqrt{18} = i\sqrt{2} + i\sqrt{(9)(2)} = i\sqrt{2} + 3i\sqrt{2}$

       $= 4i\sqrt{2}$ answer (4)

Example: What is the sum of $\sqrt{-2}$ and $\sqrt{-18}$ to the nearest thousandth ?

      (1) $6.000i$ (3) $7.071i$

      (2) $4.472i$ (4) $5.657i$

Solution: Press **2nd** x^2 [this is $\sqrt{\ }$ ( ]
           Press **(-)** **2** **)** **+**
           Press **2nd** x^2
           Press **(-)** **1** **8** **)**   **ENTER**

           Calculator gives: $5.656854249i$ answer $5.657i$ or (4)

---

1. Simplify the radical expression: show your work.

$$\sqrt{-45\ x^4\ y^7}$$

---

2. Simplify: $5\sqrt{-18} + \sqrt{-50} - i\sqrt{-75}$

Use rational exponents on real numbers and all operations on complex numbers (continued)

REMEMBER   Absolute value of complex numbers

The absolute value: $|a + bi| = \sqrt{a^2 + b^2}$

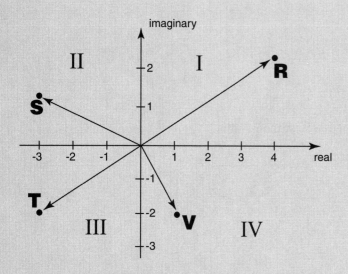

R	(4 + 2i)	Quad I
S	(-3 + i)	Quad II
T	(-3 - 2i)	Quad III
V	(1 - 2i)	Quad IV

Example: Find the distance of the point -6 + 3i from the origin.

Solution: *method 1*

$$\text{distance} = \sqrt{(-6)^2 + (3)^2} = \sqrt{45} = 3\sqrt{5} \quad \text{ans}$$

```
abs( ⁻6+3i )
        6.708203932
√(45)
        6.708203932
3√(5)
        6.708203932
■
```

Solution: *method 2* (TI-83 PLUS)

The absolute value of a complex number is the magnitude or modulus. A complex number can be shown as a vector which has both magnitude and direction.

Example: Given the complex number (-6 + 3*i*),
Press **MATH** press cursor to highlight **CPX.**
Press **5** to select abs(Press **(-)** key   Type in   **6 + 3i)**
[Note: *i* is **2nd.**] Press **ENTER**   We see 6.708203932

UNIT 3
OPERATIONS

Use rational exponents on real numbers and all operations on complex numbers (continued)

If a, b, c, and d denote real numbers, then
(a + bi) + (c + di) = (a + c) + (b + d)i.
The *x*-axis is the REAL-axis and the *y*-axis is the IMAGINARY-axis.

Example: **a**   On the complex coordinate axes, using vectors, represent
the following complex numbers, r, s, t where
r = 4 + 3i, s = 5 - 5i, and t = -6 + 6i.
b   Show graphically the vector sum r + s.
c   Show graphically the vector difference t - r.

Solution: **b**   r + s = (4 + 3i) + (5 - 5i) = (4 + 5) + (3 - 5)i = 9 - 2i
c   t - r = (-6 + 6i) - (4 + 3i) = -10 + 3i

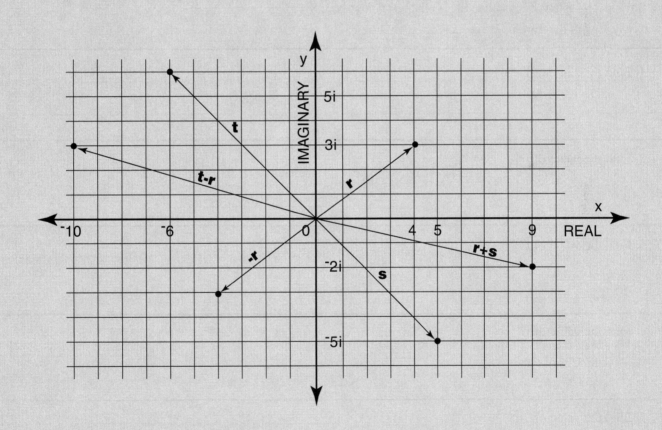

75

UNIT 3
OPERATIONS

Use rational exponents on real numbers and all operations on complex numbers (continued)

REMEMBER   Cyclical nature of the powers of i.

If the exponent is 4 or larger, divide the exponent by 4 and find the remainder below.

$i^0 = 1$

$i^1 = i$

$i^2 = -1$

$i^3 = -i$

Remainder	Value of i^x
0	+ 1
1	i
2	- 1
3	-i

Example: Find the value of i^{27}.

Solution: When 27 is divided by 4, the remainder is 3.
Therefore $i^{27} = -i$ ans.

---

1. Find the value of i^{50}

2. Find the value of i^{51}

3. Find the value of i^{52}

4. Find the value of i^{53}

5. Find the value of $7i^9$

6. Find the value of $6i^{40} - 8i^{100}$

UNIT 3
OPERATIONS

Use rational exponents on real numbers and all operations on complex numbers (continued)

REMEMBER   To solve quadratic equations by factoring, follow these steps:

1. Put the quadratic equation in descending order.
2. Move all terms from the right side to the left side of the equation.
3. Factor the leftside of the equation.
4. Set each factor equal to zero.
5. Solve each linear equation.

Example: What is the positive root of the equation $x^2 = 12 + x$?

Solution: $x^2 - x - 12 = 0$ (steps 1 and 2)

$$(x - 4)(x + 3) = 0 \qquad \text{Factor}$$

$$x - 4 = 0 \qquad x + 3 = 0 \qquad \text{Set each factor equal to zero}$$

$$x = 4 \qquad\qquad x = -3 \qquad \text{Solve}$$

$$x = 4$$

answer   reject $x = -3$

REMEMBER   To solve quadratic equations by the quadratic formula, follow these steps:

1. Put the quadratic equation into the standard form of $ax^2 + bx + c = 0$.

2. Substitute the values for a, b, and c into the quadratic formula.

$$x = \frac{-b \pm \sqrt{b^2 - 4ac}}{2a}$$

3. Solve the equation for the two values of x.

Example 1: Find the roots of the equation $2x^2 - 3 = -9x$

Solution 1: $2x^2 + 9x - 3 = 0$ Step 1

$$a = 2 \quad b = 9 \quad c = -3$$

$$x = \frac{-9 \pm \sqrt{(9)^2 - 4\,(2)(-3)}}{2(2)} = \frac{-9 \pm \sqrt{81 + 24}}{4} \qquad \text{Step 2}$$

$$x = \frac{-9 + \sqrt{105}}{4} \quad \text{and} \quad x = \frac{-9 - \sqrt{105}}{4} \qquad \text{Step 3}$$

Example 2:

Solve the equation $2x^2 - 3x = -3$ and express the roots in a + bi form.

Solution 2:

$$2x^2 - 3x + 3 = 0$$

$$a = 2$$
$$b = -3$$
$$c = 3$$

$$x = \frac{-b \pm \sqrt{b^2 - 4ac}}{2a}$$

$$x = \frac{3 \pm \sqrt{9 - 4\,(2)(3)}}{2(2)} = \frac{3 \pm \sqrt{-15}}{4}$$

$$x = \frac{3}{4} + \frac{i\sqrt{15}}{4} \quad \text{and} \quad x = \frac{3}{4} - \frac{i\sqrt{15}}{4}$$

Use rational exponents on real numbers and all operations on complex numbers (continued)

REMEMBER   Zero, Negative and Fractional Exponents Evaluated

Any Non-zero expression with a zero exponent is equivalent to one.

Examples:

| $8^0 = 1$ | $(3x)^0 = 1$ | $(3x^2 + 5x + 7)^0 = 1$ |

Any expression with a fractional exponent is equivalent to the root of the denominator raised to the numerator's power.

Examples:

| $16^{\frac{3}{4}} = \left(\sqrt[4]{16}\right)^3 = 2^3 = 8$ | $243^{\frac{2}{5}} = \left(\sqrt[5]{243}\right)^2 = 3^2 = 9$ |

Any expression with a negative exponent is equivalent to the reciprocal of the expression with a positive exponent.

Examples:

| $5^{-2} = \dfrac{1}{5^2} = \dfrac{1}{25}$ | $\dfrac{y^{-3}}{x^{-4}} = \dfrac{x^4}{y^3}$ | $64^{\frac{-1}{2}} = \dfrac{1}{64^{\frac{1}{2}}} = \dfrac{1}{8}$ |

1. Simplify the given expression using only *positive* exponents:

$$\left(\frac{81\ x^8\ y^{-2}}{x^{-12}}\right)^{\frac{1}{2}}$$

2. Simplify the given expression using only *negative* exponents:

$$\left(\frac{256\ x^9\ y^{36}}{x^{-3}}\right)^{\frac{-3}{4}}$$

3. Simplify: $2x^0 + (3x)^0 + 4^0 - 5x^{-1} + (6x)^{-1}$ where $x = 5$.

UNIT 4
MODELING/MULTIPLE REPRESENTATION

Circular functions of real numbers

REMEMBER

The unit circle, $x^2 + y^2 = 1$, has its center at (0, 0) and it's radius, $r = 1$ unit.

The direction of the velocity vector, at every instant, is the direction tangent to the circle.

$$x = r \cos \theta \qquad\qquad y = r \sin \theta \qquad\qquad x^2 + y^2 = r^2 \qquad\qquad \text{[Pythagorean theorem]}$$

$$(r \cos \theta)^2 + (r \sin \theta)^2 = r^2 \qquad\qquad \text{[substitution]}$$

$$\cos^2\theta + \sin^2\theta = 1 \qquad\qquad \text{[dividing by } r^2\text{]}$$

$$\tan \theta = \frac{\sin \theta}{\cos \theta} \qquad\qquad \tan \theta = \frac{y}{r} \div \frac{x}{r} = \text{absolute value of } \frac{y}{x}$$

sin = θr where r is the radius of a circle, θ is the central angle in *radians*, and

s is the length of the arc in the same units as r. Since $r = 1$ unit in the unit circle, s = θ units.

Example 1: *Rectangle coordinates to Polar coordinates:*

Change rectangular coordinates (4, 3) into Polar coordinates.

Use θ to nearest *ten thousandth of a radian.*

Solution 1: $\theta = \tan^{-1} \dfrac{y}{x} = \tan^{-1} \dfrac{3}{4} = .6435$ radians   [set mode to Normal, Radian]

$$r = (x^2 + y^2)^{.5} = (4 \wedge 2 + 3 \wedge 2) \wedge .5 = 5$$

Polar coordinate form (r, θ):   (5, .6435) where θ is in radians. answer

or   Polar coordinate form $r \backslash \theta$:   5\.6435 where θ is in radians. answer

Example 2: *Polar coordinates to rectangular coordinates:*

Change polar coordinates (5, .6435) into rectangular coordinates.

r is in units, θ is in radians. Find x and y to the *nearest integer.* [set MODE]

Solution 2: $x = r \cos \theta$ and $y = r \sin \theta$

$x = 5 \cos (.6435)$ $\qquad\qquad$ $y = 5 \sin (.6435)$

$x = 4$ units $\qquad\qquad\qquad$ $y = 3$ units $\qquad\qquad$ (4, 3) answer

79

UNIT 4
MODELING/MULTIPLE REPRESENTATION

Circular functions of real numbers (continued)

QUADRANT II

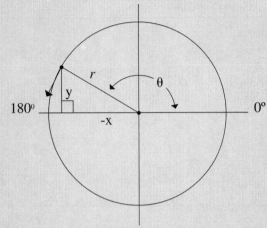

QUADRANT I

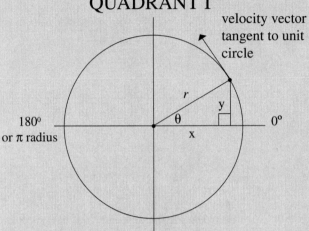

QUADRANT III

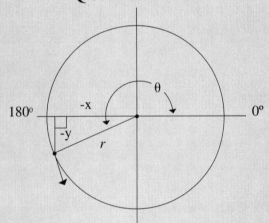

QUADRANT IV

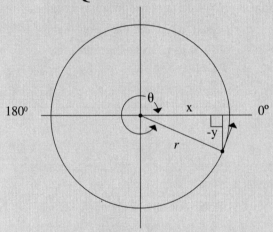

Coterminal angles: One angle is *negative*, the other angle is *positive* and the sum of the *absolute value* of the two angles *add up to 360 degrees or 2 π radians.*

Example: 30° and -330°, 90° and -270°, 130° and -230°, 180° and -180°

210° and -150°, 270° and -90°, 330° and -30°, 360° and 0°, -360° and 0°

π radians and - π radians, ½ π radians and -3/2 π radians, 1.3 radians and -.7 radians

Circular functions of *imaginary* numbers:

$x = r \cos \theta$ $y = r \sin \theta$ $x + iy = r(\cos \theta + i \sin \theta)$

Example 1: Change 3 + 4i into polar form.

Solution 1: $r = 5$, tan θ = absolute value of $\dfrac{y}{x} = \dfrac{4}{3}$, θ = 53°   5(cos 53° + i sin 53°)   answer

Example 2: Change 5(cos 53° + i sin 53°) into a complex number.

Solution 2: $r = 5$, θ = 53°, $x = 5 \cos 53°$, $y = 5 \sin 53°$, $x + iy = 5(\cos 53° + i \sin 53°) = 3 + 4i$. answer

UNIT 4
MODELING/MULTIPLE REPRESENTATION

Exponential Functions

REMEMBER

An exponential function is in the form $f(x) = ab^x$ where $a > 0$, $b > 0$, and $b \neq 1$

Press **Y=** key   Under Plot 1 to the right of

\Y1 = Type **4^x**

\Y2 = Type $\left(\frac{1}{4}\right)$**^x**

Press **ZOOM** key   Press **4** key

Note that the two graphs are reflections of each other about the *y*-axis.

Moving the cursor keys show that the two graphs *intersect at point (0, 1)*.

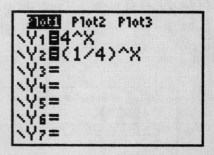

Press **Y=** key

Clear the two above functions.

\Y1 = Type   **log(x)/log(4)**

         [inverse of $f(x) = 4^x$]

\Y2 = Type   **log(x)/log($\frac{1}{4}$)**

         [inverse of $f(x) = (\frac{1}{4})^x$]

Press **ZOOM** key   Press **4** key

Note that the two graphs are reflections of each other about the x-axis.

Moving the cursor keys show that the two graphs *intersect at point (1, 0)*.

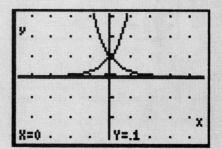

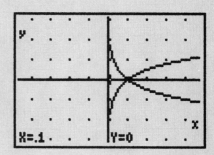

Exponential Functions (continued)

Press **Y=** key

Clear the two above functions.

\Y1 = Type **4^x**

\Y2 = **log(x)/log(4)**

Press **ZOOM** key   Press **4** key

Note that the two graphs are inverses and are reflected over the line $y = x$.

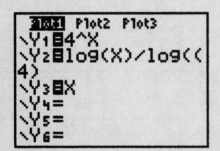

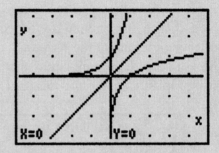

The function $f(x) = (\frac{1}{4})^x$ is an example of exponential decay such as the electrical discharge of a capacitor in a TV circuit.

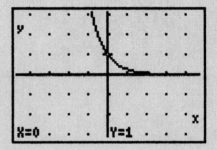

The function $f(x) = \log(x)/\log(4) + 2$ is an example of exponential build-up. A piece of steel can be stretched a certain amount and then it reaches its breaking point.

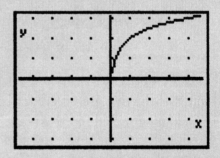

UNIT 4
MODELING/MULTIPLE REPRESENTATION

Exponential Functions (continued)

REMEMBER

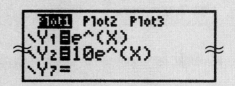

Comparing different positive *coefficients*

Press **Y=** key, move cursor and press **CLEAR**

Enter to right of \$Y_1 = e\^(x)$ [**2nd LN x)**]

Enter to right of \$Y_2 = 10e\^(x)$ [**10 2nd LN x)**]

Press **ZOOM** key   Press **4**   [selects Zdecimal]

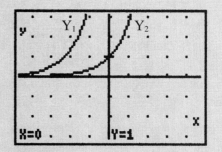

The larger coefficient results in a steeper increase for Y_2.

Comparing different negative *coefficients*

Press **Y=** key, move cursor and press **CLEAR**

Enter to right of \$Y_1 = -e\^(x)$ [**(-) 2nd LN x)**]

Enter to right of \$Y_2 = -10e\^(x)$ [**(-) 10 2nd LN x)**]

Press **ZOOM** key   Press **4**   [selects Zdecimal]

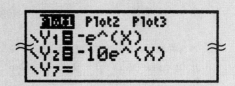

The more negative coefficient causes a steeper decrease for Y_2.

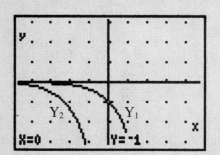

Comparing positive and negative *coefficients*

Press **Y=** key, move cursor and press **CLEAR**

Enter to right of \$Y_1 = e\^(x)$ [**2nd LN x)**]

Enter to right of \$Y_2 = -e\^(x)$ [**(-) 2nd LN x)**]

Press **ZOOM** key   Press **4**   [selects Zdecimal]

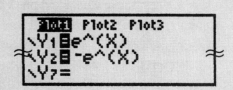

The positive coefficient graphs upward for Y_1.

The negative coefficient graphs downward for Y_2.

Note that these two functions are reflected over the x-axis.

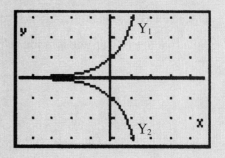

Exponential Functions (continued)

REMEMBER

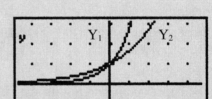

Comparing different positive *exponents*

Press **Y=** key, move cursor and press **CLEAR**

Enter to right of \Y₁ = e^(x)   [**2nd LN x)**]

Enter to right of \Y₂ = e^(.5x)   [**2nd LN .5x)**]

Press **ZOOM** key   Press **4**   [selects Zdecimal]

The larger exponent results in a steeper climb for Y₁.

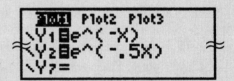

Comparing different negative *exponents*

Press **Y=** key, move cursor and press **CLEAR**

Enter to right of \Y₁ = e^(-x)   [**2nd LN (-) x)**]

Enter to right of \Y₂ = e^(-.5x)   [**2nd LN (-) .5x)**]

Press **ZOOM** key   Press **4**   [selects Zdecimal]

The more negative exponent has the faster decay for Y₁.

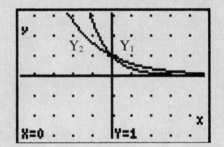

Comparing positive and negative *exponents*

Press **Y=** key, move cursor and press **CLEAR**

Enter to right of \Y₁ = e^(x)   [**2nd LN x)**]

Enter to right of \Y₂ = e^(-x)   [**2nd LN (-) x)**]

Press **ZOOM** key   Press **4**   [selects Zdecimal]

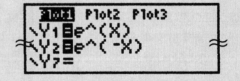

The positive exponent makes the graph increase exponentially for Y₁.

The negative exponent makes the graph decay exponentially for Y₂.

Note that these two functions are reflected over the *y*-axis.

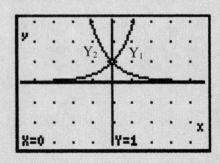

UNIT 4
MODELING/MULTIPLE REPRESENTATION

Exponential Equations

REMEMBER

To solve for x, when x is an exponent, make a substitution to make the bases equal.

Example:	Solution:
Solve for x: $9^{3x} = 27^{x-1}$	$9^{3x} = 27^{x-1}$

1. Substitute 3^2 for 9 $(3^2)^{3x} = (3^3)^{x-1}$
                 3^3 for 27

2. Simplify $3^{6x} = 3^{3x-3}$

3. Set exponents equal and solve. $6x = 3x - 3$
                                         $x = -1$ ans.

---

1. If $2^{2x-2} = 16$, find the value of x.

---

2. Find the solution set of
    $9^{x-1} = 3^x$

---

3. Find the value of x if
    $25^x = 125^2$

---

4. Solve for x:
    $7^{2x-1} = 343$

UNIT 4
MODELING/MULTIPLE REPRESENTATION

Exponential Equations (continued)

5. Solve for x:

$4^{x+3} = 16$

6. If $3^{x+1} - 5 = 22$, find the value of x.

7. The solution set of $2^{x^2+2x} = 2^{-1}$ is?

8. Solve for x:

$3^{2x+1} = 27$

9. If $11^{x^2-2x} = 11^3$, find the value(s) of x.

10. Answer true or false: (Justify your answer)

$16^2 = \left(4^4\right)^2$

Evaluating Real World Formulas

REMEMBER

Example:
A parabolic cable supports a suspension bridge
between two supports on the same level.
The maximum tension, T, in pounds
can be found using the formula:

$$T = \frac{1}{2} wa \sqrt{1 + \frac{a^2}{16d^2}}$$

If $w = 120$ lb/ft, a $= 60$ ft, and T $= 36,000$ lb
find *the deflection, d* to the *nearest hundredth* foot.

Solution:

$$T = \frac{1}{2} wa \sqrt{1 + \frac{a^2}{16d^2}}$$

$$36,000 = 0.5(120)(60) \sqrt{1 + \frac{60^2}{16d^2}}$$

Method #1:

Using **EQUATION SOLVER** in the graphing calculator,
first subtract 36,000 from both sides of the equation so that it is equal to 0.

Press **MATH** key to get the math menu
Press the number 0 key <u>or</u> move the cursor key ∨ to 0 and press the **ENTER** key
EQUATION SOLVER
EQN:0=   [is seen]
Type in $0.5 \times 120 \times 60 \times$ **2nd x^2** $1 + (60)\wedge 2 \div (16\,x\,x^2) - 36000$
You see EQUATION SOLVER
        eqn:0=.5*120*60*∨ $(1 + (60)\wedge 2/(16x^2)) - 36000$
Press **ENTER** key

the answer is seen as $x = 1.507556723$ <u>or</u> $x = 1.51$ feet to the *nearest hundredth*

UNIT 4
MODELING/MULTIPLE REPRESENTATION

Evaluating Real World Formulas (continued)

Method #2:

$$36,000 = 0.5(120)(60) \sqrt{1 + \frac{(60)^2}{16d^2}}$$

$$\frac{36,000}{0.5(120)(60)} = \sqrt{1 + \frac{(60)^2}{16d^2}}$$

$$\frac{(36,000)^2}{(0.5(120)(60))^2} = 1 + \frac{(60)^2}{16d^2}$$

$$\frac{(36,000)^2}{(0.5(120)(60))^2} - 1 = \frac{(60)^2}{16d^2}$$

$$99 = \frac{3600}{16d^2} \qquad d = 1.507556723 \text{ or } d = 1.51 \text{ feet to the } \textit{nearest hundredth.}$$

---

1. A highway engineer has to design a culvert for a small drainage ditch. The area of the upstream watershed, A, is 830 acres. She wants to find the culvert area using the formula:

   culvert area, in square foot $= C \sqrt[4]{A^3}$

   where C = 0.40 for rolling land and A is in acres.
   Show the required work to find the answer to the nearest square foot.

---

2. The magnetic field strength, H_o, due to a current carrying coil is given by the formula:

   $H_o = \dfrac{2\pi \, nI}{10r}$ where $n = 100$, the number of turns in the coil, I is the current in amperes, and $r = 2.2$, the average radius of the coil in centimeters.
   Calculate H_o to *four decimal places* when $I = 20 \times 10^{-3}$ amperes.
   Explain all calculator steps.

UNIT 4
MODELING/MULTIPLE REPRESENTATION

Evaluating Real World Formulas (continued)

3. The resale value of an automobile can be calculated using the formula $V = C(1 - r)^t$ where C is the cost of a new automobile when it is purchased, t is the number of *years* after the purchase date, and r is the rate of depreciation. If C = $30,000, and r is 20%, in how many *months* will the automobile be worth half of it's purchase price? Round your answer to the nearest *month*.

4. Bob invested $1000 in a savings bank certificate of deposit known as a CD. The CD earned 3% interest per year compounded annually. Using the formula $A = P(1 + r)^t$, how many years will it take for Bob's initial investment to *double*? P = $1000, $r = 0.03$, t = years Round your answer *up* to the nearest year.

Mike invested $1000 in a mutual fund. The mutual fund yields an equivalent interest rate of 8% per year. Using the formula above and using the answer you found for t above, find A, the amount Mike has in the mutual fund after t years. Round off to the nearest dollar.

5. The half-life of a radioactive radon gas is approximately 3.5 days. A laboratory has a 25 kilogram sample and would like to know how much of the sample will remain after 12 days. Round your answer to the *nearest tenth* of a kilogram.
Use the formula:

$$L = A(2)^{\frac{-t}{d}}$$

L is the sample size left after t days in kg
d is the half-life = 3.5 days, t = 12 days, A = 25 kg

UNIT 4
MODELING/MULTIPLE REPRESENTATION

Represent problem situations by using graphs

REMEMBER

Example:

The equation $W = 120\,I - 6\,I^2$ represents the output power (W) in watts, in a 120 volt, 20 ampere generator circuit. I is the current in amperes flowing through the circuit.
What is the maximum power, in watts, that the generator can deliver to an electrical device?
Find the current, (I), in amperes, when the power, in watts, is at maximum.

Solution:

$W = 120\,I - 6\,I^2$ is in the form of a parabola, $W = -6\,I^2 + 120\,I$.

$[\ y = Ax^2 + Bx + C\ ]$ where A = -6, B = 120, and C = 0

The equation of the axis of symmetry, $x = \dfrac{-B}{2A} = \dfrac{-120}{2(-6)} = 10$ [$I = 10$ at maximum power]

$W = 120\,I - 6\,I^2 = 120(10) - 6(10)^2$
$W = 1200 - 600 = 600$ watts maximum power.

Set W = 0 to find the roots.

$6\,I^2 - 120I = 0$

$6\,I\,(I - 20) = 0$ $I = \{\ 0,\ 20\ \}$

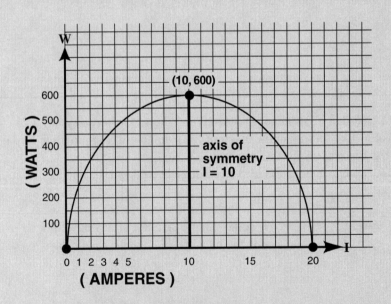

For additional practice problems on graphing conics, refer to the Westsea Publishing
SEQUENTIAL MATHEMATICS 3 Regents Exam Review Workbook pages 27 - 31,
97, 107 - 108, and 129 - 130.

UNIT 4
MODELING/MULTIPLE REPRESENTATION

Represent problem situations by using charts

1. Sarah and David are going to lease similar automobiles. Using the chart below, calculate the *cost per mile* for each person. Who will have the *lowest cost per mile*? Justify your answer.

EXPENSES	SARAH	DAVID	SARAH (per mo.)	DAVID (per mo.)
Number of months for the lease	36	36	1	1
Down payment (one time payment)	$2,016.	$324.		
Lease payment (per month)	$255.	$299.		
Sales tax paid (one time payment)	$792.	$936.		
Motor vehicles fee (per year)	$48.	$48.		
Insurance premium (per 6 months)	$702.	$804.		
Gasoline consumption (miles per gallon)	24	20		
Average cost of gasoline for 36 months (per gallon)	$1.50	$1.50		
Total cost for gasoline for 36 months (dollars)				
Maintenance (per year)	$180.	$180.		
Actual mileage driven (miles per year)	12,000	12,000		

2. Repeat problem number 1. above, using 8,000 miles for the *actual mileage driven* (per year). Keep all other values the same.

UNIT 5
MEASUREMENT

REMEMBER

Pi (π) is **not** equal to 3.14 nor $\frac{22}{7}$. Pi (π) is an **irrational** number. When we work with π in

Math B, we must us the π key on the graphing calculator for accuracy. A typical graphing calculator will use a value of $\pi = 3.1415926535898...$

Example: Solve to the nearest tenth: $50^2\pi - 40^2\pi$

Solution:
	INCORRECT	CORRECT

$50^2(3.14) - 40^2(3.14)$ $50^2(\pi) - 40^2(\pi)$

$50*50*3.14 - 40*40*3.14$ $\pi (50^2 - 40^2)$

2826 [*incorrect* answer]   2nd^ (50^2 - 40^2) ENTER

[using a graphing calculator]   2827.433388 = 2827.4 [correct answer]

[*not* using the π key]   [using a graphing calculator with the π key]

---

1. The center of a circle O is (-1, 5), and A is an endpoint of a diameter of the circle O. The coordinates of point A are (8, 5). Find the *area* of the circle to the *nearest tenth*.

---

2. The equation of a circle is $(x - 2)^2 + (y + 3)^2 = r^2$. The coordinates of an endpoint of a diameter on the circle is (2, 12). Find the value of r. Find the *area* of the circle to the *nearest tenth*.

---

3. A new federal regulation requires tire pressure monitoring on vehicles. The "indirect" system would measure the rotation of all four tires and alert the driver if the rotation of one is markedly different. A tire that is low on pressure rotates faster due to its smaller diameter, d.

  a
tire #1	tire #2	tire #3	tire #4
$d = 29$ in.	$d = 28$ in.	$d = 25$ in.	$r = 14$ in.

  Which tire is a possible problem with low air pressure? Explain your answer.

  b Find the *circumference* of the tire with the possible low pressure problem. Your answer must be to the *nearest hundredth*.

UNIT 5
MEASUREMENT

The Normal Curve and Standard Deviation

REMEMBER

Example 1:   *a*   On the normal curve below, label all values shown between - 3 and 3
           standard deviations. The mean = 500 and the standard deviation is ±100.
       b   What is the probability between - 1 and 1.5 standard deviations?
       c   What is the *minimum* value for a probability of a score in the top 15.9%?
       d   What is the *area* under the normal curve between values of 400 and 600?

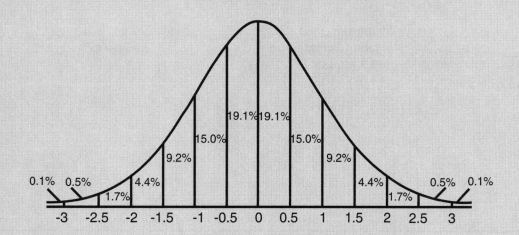

Solution 1:

a   Standard Deviation: -3   -2.5   -2   -1.5   -1   -0.5   0   0.5   1   1.5   2   2.5   3
    Values: 200 250 300 350 400 450 500 550 600 650 700   750 800

b   Looking at the normal curve between -1 and 1.5 standard deviations, we see the following:
    15% + 19.1% + 19.1% 15.0% + 9.2% = 77.4% or a probability of 0.774.

c   Looking at the right side of the normal curve, 0.1% + 0.5% + 1.7% + 4.4 + 9.2% = 15.9%.
    The minimum value has a standard deviation of 1 and the value is 600.

d   Between the values of 400 and 600 (±1 standard deviations), we see 2 times (15.0% +
    19.1%) or 68.2%. The area under the curve is the probability under the curve. In this case
    0.682 units.

    REMEMBER   The total area under the normal curve is 1. That is why the curve
    approaches the horizontal axis but does *not show it touching*. Between ±3 standard
    deviations, the probability is 100% - 0.1% - 0.1% = 99.8% = 0.998.

Example 2:   If we know the area under the normal curve to the right of a standard deviation,
                 to find the area to the left of the same standard deviation we subtract it from 1.
Solution 2:   Say the area under a normal curve to the right of 2 standard deviations from the
                 mean is 0.023, then the area to the left of the same point is 1 - 0.023 = 0.977.

UNIT 5
MEASUREMENT

The Normal Curve and Standard Deviation (continued)

1. If the test scores cluster tightly around the mean score, as they do when the group tested is relatively homogeneous, the standard deviation is smaller than it would be for a more diverse group. Given the data below, which of the four groups appear to be the most homogeneous and give an explanation.

	Nationwide Data		Student High School Year
	Math	Verbal	Sophomore
Mean, $\overline{X}$	46.1	45.5	
Standard Deviation	11.1	11.0	

	Nationwide Data		Student High School Year
	Math	Verbal	Junior
Mean, $\overline{X}$	49.3	48.4	
Standard Deviation	11.0	10.9	

2. With a mean score of 46.1 and a standard deviation of 11.1, find:

   a   the percentage of students that received a score greater than 79.4.

   b   the percentage of students that received a score between 57.2 and 68.3.

   c   the minimum score needed to be in the top 6.7% on the normal curve.

3. A person's credit rating is based on a score from 400 to 900 with the higher scores being better. If the mean score is 710 and the standard deviation is 30, find the minimum score required to place the person in the top 6.7% on the normal curve.

4. A set of normally distributed test scores in a nationwide mathematics exam yielded a mean of 49.3 and a standard deviation of 11.0. Determine the probability that a randomly selected score will be between 71.3 and 93.3.

UNIT 5
MEASUREMENT

REMEMBER

Example:

In the last quarter of 1998, Lauren invested $10,000 in an index mutual fund and Ryan invested $10,000 in a technology mutual fund. During the second quarter of 2002, Lauren's investment decreased to $9,093 while Ryan's investment increased to $12,088. Using the graph below, estimate what the results would have been during the second quarter of 2002 if both Lauren and Ryan had invested $10,000 in their mutual funds during the first quarter of the year 2000 rather than the last quarter of 1998. Round answers to the *nearest $100*.

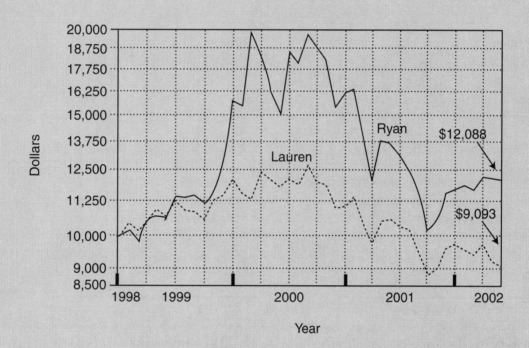

Solution:

Looking at Ryan's graph, during the 1st quarter of 2000, we see a range of $15,600 to $20,000. Looking at Lauren's graph, during the 1st quarter of 2000, we see a range of $11,300 to $12,300. Set up the ratio:

$$\frac{15,600}{12,088} = \frac{10,000}{R_{max}} \qquad \frac{20,000}{12,088} = \frac{10,000}{R_{min}} \qquad \frac{11,300}{9,093} = \frac{10,000}{L_{max}} \qquad \frac{12,3000}{9,093} = \frac{10,000}{L_{min}}$$

$$\$6,000 \leq \text{Ryan} \leq \$7,700 \qquad\qquad \$7,400 \leq \text{Lauren} \leq \$8,000$$

Conclusion: What we see here in the chart as presented by the technology mutual fund is that if a person invested money in that fund during the last quarter of 1998, he/she had some appreciation. But what the technology mutual fund does not explain is that if a person invested money in the fund during the first quarter of 2000, he/she had some depreciation, (loss). In this case, Lauren in the index fund would not do as poorly as Ryan in the technology fund. Timing is very important. Buy low and sell high.

UNIT 5
MEASUREMENT

One variable data

REMEMBER

Example:
A machine shop manufactures fender washers that must be measured for thickness by a quality control inspector. A sample batch tested gave the following measurements in millimeters:

5.0,   4.5,   4.8,   5.2,   5.5,   4.8,   5.6,   4.7,   6.2,   5.6,   6.0,   6.4,   4.8,   6.5

The company decided to *reject* any fender washers that are *at least* 3 standard deviations from the mean. Find to the *nearest tenth*, the mean, the standard deviation, and the range of thickness that are *acceptable*.

Solution:
To calculate the statistics for this data, Press **STAT**   [under edit 1:Edit is seen]
                                                    Press **1**   [L1 column is seen]
                                                    Enter **5.0** ↓   [5.000 is seen under L1]
                                                    Enter **4.5** ↓   [4.500 is seen under L1]
Enter the remaining 12 pieces of data. The bottom of the calculator screen shows L1(15) =
This tells you all 14 pieces of data have been entered under list 1.
If there are any extraneous values of data in the list, press **DEL** and the ↓ cursor until they are cleared.

Press **STAT** → to get the heading CALC
Press **1**   to get 1-Variable Stats   [1-Var Stats is seen.]
Press **2nd 1**   to select L1 list   [1-Var Stats L1 is seen.]
Press **ENTER**   to read all the 1-Var Stats

```
1-Var Stats
 x̄=5.4
 Σx=75.6
 Σx²=414.12
 Sx=.672538246
 σx=.6480740698
↓n=14
```

```
1-Var Stats
↑n=14
 minX=4.5
 Q₁=4.8
 Med=5.35
 Q₃=6
 maxX=6.5
■
```

Since some data is repeated, L1 could be the data and L2 could be the frequency. After the data and frequency have been entered, Press **STAT** → Press **1** Press **2nd 1** , **2nd 2**
This allows 1-Var Stats L1, L2 Press **Enter** to read the 1-Var Stats as above.

One variable data (continued)

REMEMBER

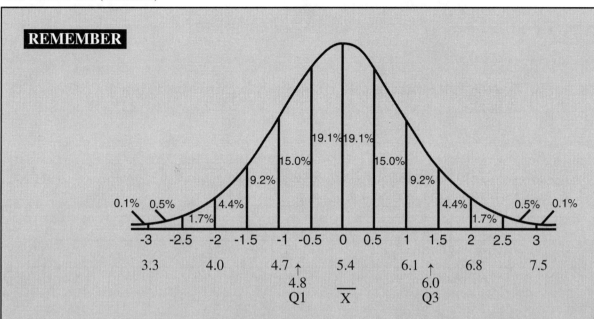

$\overline{x}$ = 5.4 mm   [mean of the 14 values of data] $\overline{x}$ = **5.4 mm Ans**

Σx = 75.6   [sum of the 14 values of data]

Σx^2 = 414.1   [sum of the x values squared]

Sx = 0.7   [*sample* standard deviation of the 14 values of data]   **Sx = 0.7 mm Ans**

σx = 0.6   [*population* standard deviation of the 14 values of data]

n = 14.0   [sample size]

min X = 4.5   [smallest of the data values]

Q1 = 4.8   [1st quartile]

Med = 5.4   [median]

Q3 = 6.0   [3rd quartile]

maxX = 6.5   [largest of the data values]

The data at 3 standard deviations is 7.5 mm. The data at -3 standard deviations is 3.3 mm. Since maxX = 6.5 mm and minX = 4.5 mm, there are no rejected fender washers.

The acceptable range is 3.4 mm to 7.4 mm which yield a range of 7.4 - 3.4 = 4.0 mm.   Ans

1. In the month of February there were 20 working days. A microprocessor manufacturer had the following number of rejected pieces for the 20 days:
   73, 93, 82, 86, 73, 88, 72, 78, 68, 75, 70, 60, 85, 86, 88, 74, 79, 92, 90, 82

   Determine the percent of rejected microprocessors that were within ± 2 standard deviations of the mean. When you compare the results with the normal curve, do they appear to approximate a normal distribution? Explain your reasoning.

UNIT 5
MEASUREMENT

Two variable data

REMEMBER

Example:

a   The table below, created in 2002, shows a history of first-class stamp rates from 1958 to 2002. On the accompanying grid, construct a *scatter plot* where the independent variable is years and the dependent variable is cents.

b   State the *linear regression equation* with the coefficient and base rounded off tho the nearest *thousandth*. Using this equation, determine the prediction that should be made for the year 2005, to the *nearest cent*.

c   Draw the *linear regression line* on the same coordinates as the scatter plot. Label 2 points.

d   Repeat b above using the *exponential regression equation*.

Year	58	63	68	71	74	75	78	81	81	85	88	91	95	99	01	02
Rate (cents)	4	5	6	8	10	13	15	18	20	22	25	29	32	33	34	37

Solution:

a   *scatter plot:*

c   *linear regression line:*

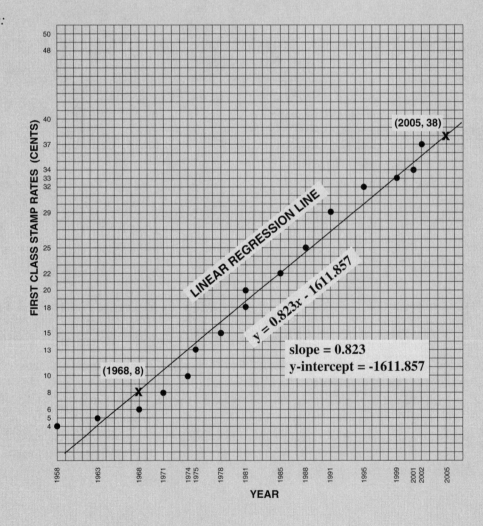

98

UNIT 5
MEASUREMENT

Two variable data (continued)

b   *Enter the data from the table.*
   Press **STAT   1**   [Edit]
   Type in the set of *x*-data values in the list L1 column.   [Use *4 digits* for the year]
   Type in the set of *y*-data values in the list L2 column.   [Rate in *cents*]
   Use the appropriate cursor key after each data entry.
   When the 16 *x*-data values are entered, you should see at the bottom left of the display
   L1(17)=
   Press the appropriate cursor keys and start entering the corresponding 16 *y*-data values in the list L2.
   When the 16 *y*-data values are entered, you should see at the bottom of the display
   L2(17)=

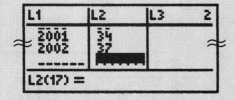

Two variable data (continued)

Press **STAT** →   [CALC]
Press **2**   [2-Var Stats]
Press **2nd 1** , **2nd 2**   [L1, L2]

```
2-Var Stats L1,L
2
```

Press **Enter** to get the 2-variable stats seen below.

```
2-Var Stats
 x̄=1981.875
 Σx=31710
 Σx²=62847986
 Sx=13.49011984
 σx=13.06175237
↓n=16
■
```

```
2-Var Stats
↑ȳ=19.4375
 Σy=311
 Σy²=7947
 Sy=11.2603656
 σy=10.90280211
↓Σxy=618610
■
```

```
2-Var Stats
↑σy=10.90280211
 Σxy=618610
 minX=1958
 maxX=2002
 minY=4
 maxY=37
```

```
2-Var Stats
↑σy=10.90280211
 Σxy=618610
 minX=1958
 maxX=2002
 minY=4
 maxY=37
LinReg(ax+b)
```

Now that the *x*-values have been stored in list L1 and the *y*-values have been stored in list L2, the regression line or line of best fit can be calculated.

Press **STAT** →   [CALC]
Press **4**   [selects the LinReg(a*x*+b) option]
Press **ENTER**   to show a summary of the line
                           LinReg(a*x*+b) statistics.

```
LinReg
 y=ax+b
 a=.8231065116
 b=-1611.856718
 r²=.9723860238
 r=.9860963563
```

REMEMBER

$y = ax + b$ is the standard equation of a straight line .
where a is the slope, b is the y-intercept, and r is the linear correlation coefficient.

The equation of the linear regression line is $y = 0.823x - 1611.857$

For the year 2005, $y = 0.823(2005) - 1611.857 = 38.258$.
For the year 2005, there is a very high correlation since r = 0.986, that the first-class postage can be estimated to be 38 cents. The scatter diagram is very close to the line of best fit.

d   Repeating part b using the *exponential regression equation*:

Press **STAT**   →   [CALC]
Press the numerical 0   [ExpReg]
"ExpReg" is seen at the bottom left of the display.
Press **ENTER**
A summary of the ExpReg option is seen.

For the year 2002, $y = (1.095 \times 10^{-44})(1.054)^x$

$y = (1.095 \times 10^{-44})(1.054)^{2002}$

$y = 58$ cents for 1st class rates in 2002.

1. Two different tests were designed to measure understanding of Math B topics. To make the two tests comparable, they were assigned different scaled scores for the same raw score.

Test x	75	74	73	72	72	71	70	69	69	68	67	66	65	64	63
Test y	74	73	71	70	69	68	67	66	65	64	63	62	60	59	58

a   Construct a scatter plot for these scores, and then write an equation for the line of best fit. Round slope and y-intercept to the *nearest hundredth*.

b   Find the correlation coefficient.

c   Predict the scaled score, to the nearest integer, on test x for a scaled score of 85 on test y.

Two variable data (continued)

1. (continued)

UNIT 5
MEASUREMENT

2. The peak electrical usage in megawatts for five summer days in the years 1997 to 2001 are shown in the accompanying table.

megawatts (y)	4310	4383	4757	4369	4906
year (x)	1997	1998	1999	2000	2001

a Determine a linear relationship for x, years, versus y, megawatts consumed, based on the data given. The data should be entered using the year with 4 digits, and electrical usage in megawatts such as (1997, 4310).

b Plot the linear relationship on the accompanying grid.

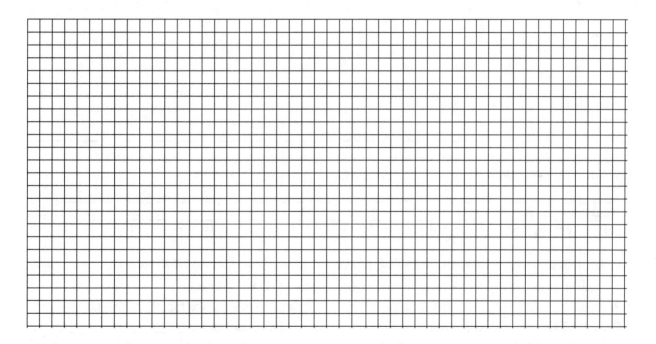

c If this relationship continues, what is the anticipated megawatts of electric consumed in the year 2010?

UNIT 5
MEASUREMENT

3. The 2002 win-loss statistics for the Major League Soccer, Eastern Division, teams on a particular day is shown in the accompanying chart.

TEAM	W	L
Metro Stars	9	10
Chicago	8	8
Columbus	8	9
New England	7	12
District of Columbia	6	11

Find the mean for the number of wins, $\overline{W}$, and the mean for the number of losses, $\overline{L}$.

Determine if the point $(\overline{W}, \overline{L})$ is a point on the line of best fit. Justify your answer.

4. An eyeglass frame manufacturer wants to limit the frame bridge size and the frame temple length to a total of 20 sizes as shown in the accompanying chart.

Bridge Size, x, mm	14	14	14	15	15	16	16	17	17	17	18	18	18	19	19	19	20	22	24	25
Temple Length, y, mm	120	125	130	125	130	125	130	125	135	140	130	135	140	130	135	140	130	140	145	150

Using a graphing calculator, and the **STAT 1** keys, enter the x values in the L1 list and the

y values in the L2 list. Press **STAT** → keys to get the "CALC" heading.

Press **2** to get the 2-Var Stats. When "2-Var Stats" is seen at the top of the display,

Press **ENTER.** Copy the following 2-Var Stats: mean $(\overline{x})$, mean $(\overline{y})$, $\overline{x} = $ _____, $\overline{y} = $ _____

Press **STAT** → to get the heading "CALC"

Press **4** to get the LinReg ($ax + b$) options.

When you see LinReg ($ax + b$) at the bottom of the display,

Press **ENTER** Write the LinReg results: $y = ax + b$

slope = _____, y-intercept = _____, correlation coefficient = _____

Write the equation of the linear regression line: _____

Predict a temple length, y, that corresponds to a bridge size, $x = 21$. (nearest integer)

$y = $ _____, ordered pair $(21, $ ____ $)$

UNIT 5
MEASUREMENT

Central angles and length of arcs in a circle

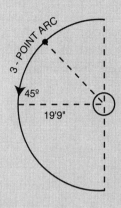

REMEMBER

Example
The 3-point arc in a college basketball court is
19 feet 9 inches from the center of the basketball rim.
A basketball player dribbles along this arc.
What distance has the basketball player moved if the
subtended arc is 45°? Express your answer to the
nearest *tenth of a foot.*

Solution *Method 1:*

A central angle is measured by its subtended arc. Therefore the central angle is 45°. The radius
of the circle is 19 feet 9 inches. If *l* is the length of the arc in inches, *C* is the circumference of
the circle in inches, and *n* is the number of degrees in the central angle, we can use the following
proportion:

$$\frac{l \text{ in.}}{C \text{ in.}} = \frac{n°}{360°} \qquad \frac{l}{2\pi r} = \frac{n°}{360°} \qquad \frac{l}{2\pi(237)} = \frac{45}{360}$$

$l = 186.139$ inches $= 15.512$ feet   The <u>basketball player dribbled 15.5 feet</u>.

Solution *Method 2:*
We can use the formula: $S = \theta r$ where S is the length of the arc in the *same units* as the

radius, r. θ is the central angle measured in *radians*. $45° = \frac{45\pi}{180}$ radians $= 0.785$ radians.

$S = \theta r = 0.785(237) = 186.045$ inches $= 15.504$ feet   Answer: <u>15.5 feet</u>

NOTE: In making calculations, we see different raw answers above. This is due to the number of
digits stored by the calculator and not seen on the screen. This is called breakage.

1. A basketball player throws the basketball to score
   a 3-pointer. The ball lands on the rim and rolls on it
   before it drops in. What distance has the basketball
   rolled when the subtended arc is 210°?
   Express your answer to the nearest *tenth of an inch.*

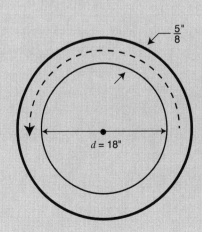

UNIT 6
UNCERTAINTY

Probability and statistics.

Example 1. Kia solves a quadratic equation. Using her calculator she sees that the roots are real, rational, and equal. Kia Knows the discriminant is

        (1) zero   (3) a perfect square

        (2) negative   (4) not a perfect square

Solution 1: $b^2 - 4ac = 0$ in order for the roots to be real, rational, and equal.

       Answer. (1) zero

Example 2. The relationship between a women's weight and her height is given by the accompanying table.

Height (inches)	60	61	62	63	64	65
Weight (pounds)	98	104	112	122	130	140

What is the linear correlation coefficient for this relationship?

Solution 2: On the TI-83 Plus, first clear your list.
STAT Enter L1, 60 enter, 61 Enter, 62 Enter, 63 Enter, 64 Enter, 65 Enter $\rightarrow \uparrow$
L$_2$, 98 Enter, 104 Enter, 112 Enter, 122 Enter, 130 Enter, 140 Enter
STAT $\rightarrow$ CALC 4 [LinReg ax + b] Enter.

What will appear is

        LinReg

        $y = ax + b$

        $a = 8.514285714$

        $b = -414.4761905$

        $r_2 = .9947427377$

        $r = .9973679049$

Answer. $r = .9973679049$ this is the linear correlation coefficient

Probability and statistics (continued)

 **REMEMBER**

Solution 2: (continued)

Press **2nd O** [catalog]

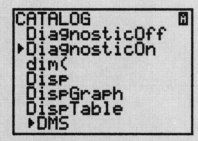

Press ENTER

Press **ENTER**

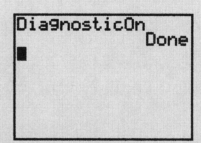

Press **STAT 1** [Edit]

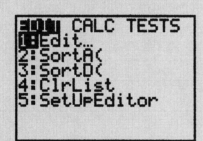

Enter data & Press **ENTER** each time

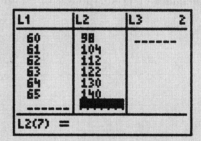

Press **STAT** → 4

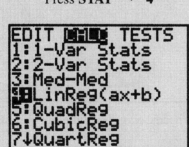

Press **ENTER**

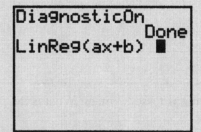

Final results shown

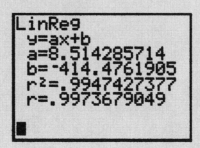

UNIT 6
UNCERTAINTY

Probability (exactly, at most ≤, at least ≥)

1. At a certain intersection, the light for northbound traffic is red for 35 seconds, yellow for 5 seconds, and green for 60 seconds. To the nearest tenth, what is the probability that out of the next 10 northbound cars that arrive randomly at the light, _exactly_ 4 will be stopped by a red light?

2. Ed Baron can hit a home run 8% of the time. What is the probability he will hit, _exactly_ two home runs in ten at bats?

3. A fair coin is tossed 7 times. What is the probability it lands heads, _exactly_ 4 times?

UNIT 6
UNCERTAINTY

Probability (exactly, at most ≤, at least ≥)(continued)

4. The Mets are playing the Braces 4 times. If the probability that the Mets win a game is $\frac{3}{5}$, what is the probability the Mets win *at most* 2 games?

5. The Barons will play the Jays six times. The probability the Barons win a game is $\frac{2}{3}$. What is the probability the Barons will win *at most* two games?

6. As shown in the accompanying diagram, a circular target with a radius of 10 inches, has a ring formed by an outer radius of 4 inches and an inner radius of 2 inches. If 6 darts randomly hit the target, what is the probability *at most* 2 darts hit the ring?

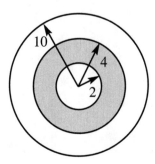

UNIT 6
UNCERTAINTY

Normal distribution, mean, standard deviation

1. A set of normally distributed student test scores has a mean of 77 and a standard deviation of 8. What is the probability that a randomly selected score will be between 73 and 89?

2. In Mr. Bower's Math class 256 students took the Math final exam. The scores were normally distributed with a mean of 76.5 and a standard deviation of 11.6. How many students failed the exam?

3. In his trigonometry classes, Mr. Bee predicts that 12 out of 70 students will get scores of 85 or higher on an exam with a normal distribution. The mean score is 80, with a standard deviation of 5. Was his prediction correct? If yes, describe how you arrived at your conclusion. If not, what should he have predicted to be more precise?

4. A set of normally distributed student test scores has a mean of 81 and a standard deviation of 6. What is the probability that a randomly selected score will be between 72 and 90?

UNIT 6
UNCERTAINTY

Normal distribution, mean, standard deviation (continued)

5. In a College Calculus course there are 420 students. Their scores on the final examination are normally distributed with a mean of 75.2 and a standard deviation of 8.2. How many students are expected to receive a grade between 79 and 84?

6. The scores on a 100 point exam are normally distributed with a mean of 72 and standard deviation of 8. A student's score places him between the 84th and 85th percentile. Which of the following best represents his score.

     (1) 77   (3) 85

     (2) 81   (4) 89

7. A survey of the candy eating habits of sixth grade students in Westbury Middle School revealed the mean number of packages of candy per sixth grader was 16 packages with a standard deviation of 4. If a normal distribution is assumed, find an interval that approximately 95% of the student population of the Middle School will eat packages of candy. Explain your answer.

UNIT 6
UNCERTAINTY

Normal distribution, mean, standard deviation (continued).

8. Eighteen seniors took a Math examination and received the following scores:

   73, 63, 72, 65, 88, 89, 75, 69, 85, 91, 85, 70, 77, 82, 83, 79, 93, 95.

   Determine what percent of the students scored within one standard deviation of the mean.

   Do the results of the examination approximate a normal distribution? Justify your answer.

9. A survey of the study habits of the population in Westbury High School revealed the mean number of hours a student studied each week was 18 hours, with a standard deviation of 4. If a normal distribution is assumed, find an interval that contains the total number of hours that 86.6% of the students study.

UNIT 6
UNCERTAINTY

Entering data under lists L1 and L2 in a graphing calculator, line of best fit.

1. Given X = {1,2,3,4,5,6} and Y = {120, 80, 20, 0, -15, -25}, where X is in miles above sea level and Y is the temperature in °F at that height. Find the equation that best fits the data.
    Determine the height when the temperature is -40.

2. The 2002 win-loss statistics for the National League East baseball teams on a particular date is shown in the accompanying chart.

Team	W	L
Atlanta	32	26
Mets	29	28
Florida	29	29
Montreal	28	30
Philadelphia	23	33

    Find the mean for the number of wins, $\overline{W}$, and the mean for the number of losses, $\overline{L}$, and determine if the point $(\overline{W}, \overline{L})$ is a point on the line of best fit.
    Justify your answer.

UNIT 6
UNCERTAINTY

Entering data under lists L1 and L2 in a graphing calculator, line of best fit (continued).

3. The table below shows the relationship between the number of deer and the average temperature for a given year. (The colder it is, the less food is available and therefore less deer survive.)

Number of deer (N)	Average Temp (F°)
11,000	25°
12,000	30°
13,500	34°
14,900	37°
17,000	40°

Find the mean for the number of deer $\overline{N}$ and there average temp. $\overline{T}$. Determine if the point $(\overline{N}, \overline{T})$ is on the line of best fit. Justify your answer. Could you find another curve to better justify your answer?

4. The points on the scatter plot below represent the amount of rain fall during the year 2002 in Bangor Maine.

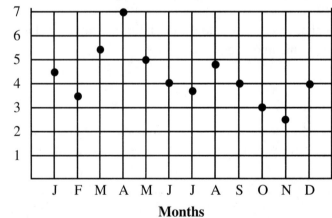

Months

(1) There is a positive correlation.   (3) There is a negative correlation.

(2) There is a zero correlation.   (4) There is no correlation.

UNIT 6
UNCERTAINTY

Scatter plots, correlation coefficient, regression lines, predictions

5. A chart of students' grades in a mathematic course and the corresponding hours spent on homework is shown.

Hours Spent on Homework	Grade in a Mathematics Course
0	55
0.5	65
1.0	77
1.5	81
2.0	90
2.5	88

Draw a *scatter plot*.

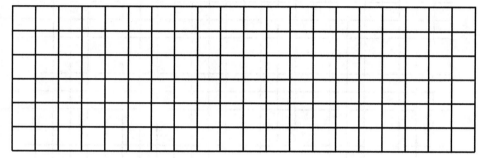

What is the equation for the *linear regression line*? Justify your answer.

Find the *linear correlation coefficient*. Justify your answer.

6. The relationship between the height of a man and his chest size is given by the following table:

Height (inches)	70	71	72	73	74
Chest Size (inches)	42	44	45	46	46

Find the *linear correlation coefficient for* this data. Justify your answer.

UNIT 6
UNCERTAINTY

Scatter plots, correlation coefficient, regression lines, predictions (continued)

7. Two different tests were designed to measure the knowledge of a certain math skill. The two tests (test A and test B) were given to twelve students with the following results.

test A	67	91	73	82	88	54	84	61	94	71	75	86
test B	65	90	75	74	90	61	85	73	97	72	80	86

Construct a *scatter plot* for these scores, and then write an equation for the *line of best fit* (round the slope and the y-intercept to the nearest hundredth).

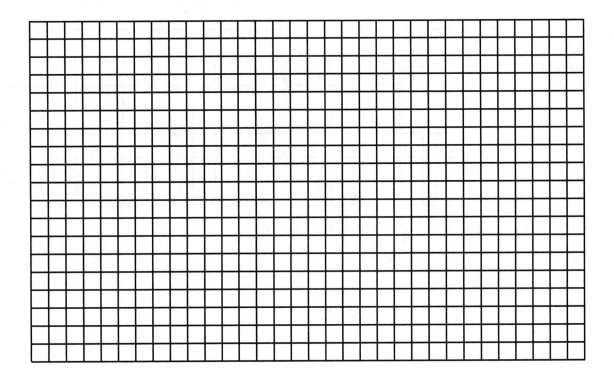

Find the *correlation coefficient.*

Predict the score, to the *nearest integer*, on test B for a student who scored 89 on test A.

Scatter plots, correlation coefficient, regression lines, predictions (continued)

8. The availability of crude oil in Texas is decreasing as shown in the accompanying table.

Year (x)	1992	1994	1996	1998	2000	2002
Gallons (y)	450	390	340	285	240	192

[Oil is in hundred thousand gallons]

Determine a linear relationship for x (years) versus y (gallons), based on the data given. The data should be entered using the year and gallons available (in hundred thousands), such as (1992, 450).

If this relationship continues, determine the number of gallons of oil available in Texas in the year 2007?

If this relationship continues, during what year will oil first become unavailable in Texas?

9. On a standardized test, the distribution of scores is normal. The mean of the scores is 72 and the standard deviation is 4.6. If a student scored 78, what percentile would the score rank nearest? Justify your answer.

UNIT 6
UNCERTAINTY

Permutations (n Pr), Combinations (n Cr)

Permutations

REMEMBER

Use permutations when *arranging* objects into a specific order, without repetition.

(AB is not the same as BA)

The number of *arrangements* of n different objects, taken r at a time is represented by nPr

$$n\text{P}n = n!, \quad n\text{P}_1 = n \quad \text{and} \quad n\text{P}r = \frac{n!}{(n-r)!}$$

Example 1: How many three-letter arrangements can be formed from the letters of the word PICTURE?

Solution 1: $7\text{P}3 = 7 \bullet 6 \bullet 5 \bullet = 210$ different three-letter *arrangements*

Example 2: How many eight-letter *arrangements* can be formed from the letters of the word REMEMBER?

Solution 2: $\dfrac{8\text{P}8}{3! \bullet 2! \bullet 2!} \qquad \dfrac{8 \bullet 7 \bullet 6 \bullet 5 \bullet 4 \bullet 3 \bullet 2 \bullet 1}{3 \bullet 2 \bullet 1 \bullet 2 \bullet 1 \bullet 2 \bullet 1} = 1680$ eight-letter arrangements

Combinations

REMEMBER

Use combinations when order is *not* important or when making a *selection*.

(AB is the same as BA)

Formula: $\dbinom{n}{r} = n\text{C}r = \dfrac{n\text{P}r}{r!} = \dfrac{n!}{r!(n-r)!}$

Example 1: How many different 3 person committees can be *selected* from 7 people?

Solution 1: $\dbinom{7}{3} = 7\text{C}3 = \dfrac{7\text{P}3}{3!} = \dfrac{7 \bullet 6 \bullet 5}{3 \bullet 2 \bullet 1} = 35$ *different committees*

Example 2: From a group of 5 boys and 7 girls, how many 4 person subcommittees can be *selected* if it must consist of exactly 2 boys and 2 girls?

Solution 2: $(5\text{C}2) \bullet (7\text{C}2) = \left(\dfrac{5 \bullet 4}{2 \bullet 1}\right)\left(\dfrac{7 \bullet 6}{2 \bullet 1}\right) = 210$ *different committees*

Remember: $n\text{C}_0 = 1, \quad n\text{C}n = 1 \quad \text{and} \quad n\text{C}r = n\text{C}n{-}r$

UNIT 6
UNCERTAINTY

Σ notation problems

REMEMBER

Example:

Find the value of $\displaystyle\sum_{r=2}^{5} (r^2 - 1)$

Solution: $\displaystyle\sum_{r=2}^{5} (r^2 - 1) = (2^2 - 1) + (3^2 - 1) + (4^2 - 1) + (5^2 - 1) = 50$ answer

---

1. Find the value of $\displaystyle\sum_{n=1}^{4} (3n + 2)^{n-1}$

---

2. Find the value of $\displaystyle\sum_{k=0}^{3} 0.5\,k$

---

3. Find the value of $\displaystyle\sum_{m=3}^{6} \frac{m^2}{5}$

---

4. Find the value of $\displaystyle\sum_{p=3}^{7} (p - 2)^2$

---

5. Find the value of $\displaystyle\sum_{r=0}^{2} {}_4C_r$ where ${}_nC_r$ represents the number of combinations of n items taken r at a time.

Application in algebra

REMEMBER

Example: A telephone company offers several monthly telephone calling plans.

PLAN	MONTHLY CHARGE	COST PER MINUTE
A	none	90 cents
B	$10	50 cents
C	$40	10 cents

a   How many calls must you make for Plan B to be cheaper than Plan A?

b   How many calls must you make for Plan C to be cheaper than Plan A?

c   How many calls must you make for Plan C to be cheaper than Plan B?

Solution: Let n = number of calls per month. Convert the monthly charge to cents.

Plan A: $0 + 90n$ Plan B: $1000 + 50n$ Plan C: $4000 + 10n$

a
$$\text{Plan B} < \text{Plan A}$$
$$1000 + 50n < 0 + 90n$$
$$1000 < 40n$$
$$n > 25$$

b
$$\text{Plan C} < \text{Plan A}$$
$$4000 + 10n < 0 + 90n$$
$$4000 < 80n$$
$$n > 50$$

c
$$\text{Plan C} < \text{Plan B}$$
$$4000 + 10n < 1000 + 50n$$
$$3000 < 40n$$
$$n > 75$$

Plan A: $Y_1 = 90n$

Plan B: $Y_2 = 50n + 1000$

Plan C: $Y_3 = 10n + 4000$

Note: The three cost functions could be put on a graph and comparisons made to arrive at the same results.

UNIT 6
UNCERTAINTY

Applications in algebra (continued)

1. It costs $40 to rent a car for one day and 20 cents for each mile. If *x* represents the miles traveled on a given day, in terms of *x*, write an expression which would represent the cost of renting the car for one day.

2. During a Thanksgiving day sale, a store will give a 25% discount for every purchase made all day long and an additional 10% on the *discounted cost* for every purchase made between 10 a.m. and 12 noon. If a purchase of *d* dollars is made at 11 a.m., write an expression in terms of *d*, that you would pay for a purchase.

3. On a trip to Lake Meade, the Faulke family averaged 40 mph and on their return trip home along the same route they averaged 60 mph. What was their average speed in mph for the round trip? Justify your answer.

4. The cost to deliver a letter by messenger is a flat fee for the first 3 ounces and a per ounce fee for each additional ounce above 3 ounces. If a 7 ounce letter costs $6.90 to deliver and a 14 ounce letter costs $11.10 to deliver to the same address, find the cost of a 20 ounce letter to the same address. Justify your answer.

UNIT 6
UNCERTAINTY

5. A communications company has two pricing plans. Plan #1 charges $15 a month and $0.10 per minute for transmitting data. Plan #2 charges $25 a month and $0.08 per minute for transmitting data. Calculate the number of minutes used per month that would make both plans cost the same for the month. Show the required work.

6. A certain strain of bacteria doubles every 20 minutes. The formula to determine the number of bacteria after t hours can be determined by the formula: $B = 10,000(2)^{3t}$.
   Determine the number of bacteria, B, available in 2 hours.

7. The Banks family wants to invest $5000 for their child's future college expenses.
   If they invest it at 3.25% with interest compounded 4 times per year, determine the value of the account, *in dollars*, after 10 years.

   Use the formula $A = P\left(1 + \frac{r}{n}\right)^{nt}$ where A = value of the investment after t years
   P = principal invested, r = annual interest rate,
   and n = number of times compounded per year.

8. The Stockman family wants to invest $2500 for their child's future college expenses.
   If they invest it at 12% with interest compounded annually, determine the value of the account, *in dollars*, after 10 years.

   Use the formula $A = P\left(1 + \frac{r}{n}\right)^{nt}$ where A = value of the investment after t years
   P = principal invested, r = annual interest rate,
   and n = number of times compounded per year.

   When you compare the answers for problems 7 and 8, the larger value of A is due to:

   (1) P   (3) n

   (2) r (4) t

Applications in algebra (continued)

9. A computer store wants to calculate the break-even point where cost, C, is equal to sales, S.
   The owner uses the formula: P = S − C where
   P is the profit in dollars, S is the sales in dollars, and
   C is the costs in dollars.
   The cost, C, of selling x computers in the store is modeled by the equation:

   $$C = \frac{3,200,000}{x} + 84,000$$

   The store sales, S, for selling x computers is modeled by the equation:

   $$S = 500x$$

   To find the break-even point, what should the profit, P, be equal to?

   Find the minimum number of computers that have to be sold for the sales to equal to or greater than the costs.

UNIT 7
PATTERNS/FUNCTIONS

Patterns

REMEMBER

Example: The surface area of a sphere is $S = 4\pi r^2$ and the volume is $V = \frac{4\pi r^3}{3}$.

Express the volume as a function of the surface area.

Solution: $S = 4\pi r^2$, $\frac{S}{4\pi} = r^2$, $r = \sqrt{\frac{S}{4\pi}}$

$$V = \frac{4}{3}\pi r^3 \quad = \frac{4}{3}\pi \left(\sqrt{\frac{S}{4\pi}}\right)3 \quad = \frac{4}{3}\pi \frac{S}{4\pi}\sqrt{\frac{S}{4\pi}} \quad = \frac{S}{3}\sqrt{\frac{S}{4\pi}} \qquad \text{answer}$$

---

1.   Given two lines whose equations are $4x + y - 2 = 0$ and $2x + by + 3 = 0$, determine the value of b such that the two lines will be *parallel*.

---

2.   Given two lines whose equations are $2x + y - 4 = 0$ and $-3x + by - 1 = 0$, determine the value of b such that the two lines are *perpendicular*.

UNIT 7
PATTERNS/FUNCTIONS

Functions

1. A person attached to a bungee cord jumps from a platform. When he reaches the maximum length of the bungee cord, he will oscillate according to the formula $y = 20\cos 4\pi t$.
   Find the period of the oscillation. Justify your answer.

2. If $f(x) = 2x^2 - 5$ and $g(x) = \sqrt[3]{x}$, find the value of $(g \circ f)(4)$. Justify your answer.

3. If $y = 2x - 5$, what is the inverse of this function? Show your work.

4. Find the solution set of the equation $\sqrt{x + 12} = x$ and check your answer(s).

5. a Solve for x in simplest $a + bi$ radical form: $x^2 + 5x + 10 = 0$

   b What did you notice about the two solutions for x?

   c Using a graphing calculator, solve for x in $a + bi$ form where a and b are rounded to the *nearest thousandth*.

   d How many points of intersection are there with the graph of this function and the x-axis?

UNIT 7
PATTERNS/FUNCTIONS

6. A storage container is in the shape of a rectangular box. It is 4 times as long as it is high and twice as wide as it is high. Each square foot of the bottom of the box costs $10 to build and each square foot of the top and sides of the box costs $8 to build.

   Write a function for the cost of building the container.

   Using this function, determine the dimensions of a container that would cost $15,360 to build.

7. The period of a pendulum (T), in seconds, is the length of time it takes for the pendulum to make one complete swing back and forth. The formula $T = 2\pi \sqrt{\dfrac{L}{32}}$ gives the period for a pendulum of length L in feet. If you want the pendulum to swing back and forth once every 4 sec., how long L, to the *nearest tenth* of a foot, would you make the pendulum?

Functions (continued)

8. Sketch the graph of the function $f(x) = 2.5^x$ and $g(x) = \log_{2.5} x$. Describe the relationship between $f(x)$ and $g(x)$. Give the domain and range of g.

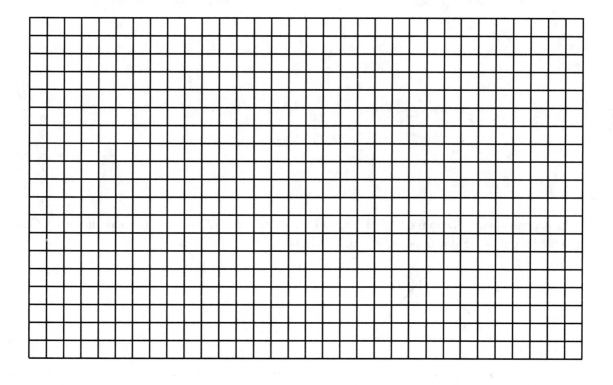

9. In the equation $y = .8(1.53^x)$, y represents the number of people in millions who exercise, and x represents the number of years since 2000. Find the year in which the number of people who exercise will be more than 30 million. (Only an algebraic solution will be accepted.)

UNIT 7
PATTERNS/FUNCTIONS

Law of sines and cosines

REMEMBER

Law of Sines: [Working with 2 sides and 2 opposite angles]

$$\frac{\text{side } a}{\text{side } b} = \frac{\sin A}{\sin B}$$

Law of Cosines: [Working with 3 sides and 1 angle]

$$c^2 = a^2 + b^2 - 2ab \cos C$$

↑   ↑
opposite each other

---

1.   In the accompanying diagram of △GHF, m∠G = 58°, m∠H = 72° and the side opposite vertex G is 12. Find the length of the side opposite vertex F and find the area of △GHF.

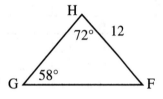

---

2.   Three houses are located as in the diagram below. House A is measured to be 200 ft. from house B. House B is measured to be 150 ft. from house C. If the angle made by AB and BC is 105°, how far is house A from house C?

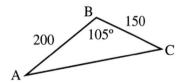

UNIT 7
PATTERNS/FUNCTIONS

Miscellaneous

---

1. Two rescue trucks try to pull a crane out of a ditch. One rescue truck applies force of 1,200 pounds while the other rescue truck applies a force of 2,000 pounds. Th resultant force is 3,000 pounds. Find the angle that the <u>resultant force makes with the 2,000 pound force</u>. Round to the *nearest degree*.

---

2. In the accompanying diagram, cabins E, F and G are located on the shore of a circular lake, and cabin H is located near the lake. Point J is a beach on the lake shore and is collinear with cabins H and G. Cabins E, F and H are also collinear. The road between cabins F and H is 10 miles long. The distance between cabins E and F is 10 miles. The road between cabin H and beach J is 8 miles. What is the distance between beach J and Cabin G. Justify your answer.

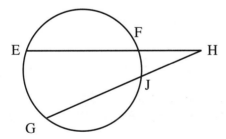

Miscellaneous

3. Is $\cos \frac{1}{2}x = \frac{1}{2}\cos x$?   Justify your answer.   Use of the grid is optional.

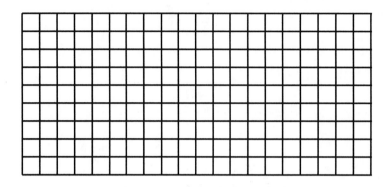

4. The graphs of two radio waves are recorded on the same oscilloscope, where $0 \leq x < 360°$. The radio waves are defined by the following functions:

$$y = 3\cos^2 x \quad \text{and} \quad y = 2 - 5\cos x$$

Find all values of x, to the *nearest degree*, for which the two radio waves are equal in the interval $0 \leq x < 360°$. [Only an algebraic solution will be accepted.]

MATHEMATICS B

Practice Regents Exams

Notice...

A graphing calculator, a straightedge (ruler), and a compass must be available for your use while talking this examination.

Formulas

Area of Triangle

$K = \frac{1}{2}ab \sin C$

Law of Cosines

$a^2 = b^2 + c^2 - 2bc \cos A$

Functions of the Sum of Two Angles

$\sin (A + B) = \sin A \cos B + \cos A \sin B$
$\cos (A + B) = \cos A \cos B - \sin A \sin B$

Functions of the Double Angle

$\sin 2A = 2 \sin A \cos A$
$\cos 2A = \cos^2 A - \sin^2 A$
$\cos 2A = 2 \cos^2 A - 1$
$\cos 2A = 1 - 2 \sin^2 A$

Functions of the Difference of Two Angles

$\sin (A - B) = \sin A \cos B - \cos A \sin B$
$\cos (A - B) = \cos A \cos B + \sin A \sin B$

Functions of the Half Angle

$\sin \frac{1}{2}A = \pm\sqrt{\dfrac{1 - \cos A}{2}}$

$\cos \frac{1}{2}A = \pm\sqrt{\dfrac{1 + \cos A}{2}}$

Law of Sines

$\dfrac{a}{\sin A} = \dfrac{b}{\sin B} = \dfrac{c}{\sin C}$

Normal Curve

Standard Deviation

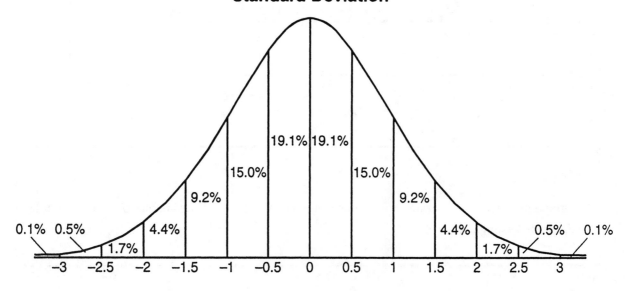

Part I

Answer all questions in this part. Each correct answer will receive 2 credits. No partial credit will be allowed. Record your answer in the spaces provided on the separate answer sheet. [40]

Use this space for computations.

1 Which relation is *not* a function?

   (1) $y = |x|$ (3) $y = 2x^2 - 3x - 1$

   (2) $y = 2 \cos 3x$ (4) $x^2 - y^2 = 16$

2 What is the domain of $g(x) = \sqrt{x^2 - x - 6}$?

   (1) $\{x \mid x \le -3 \text{ or } x \ge -2\}$ (3) $\{x \mid -2 \le x \le 3\}$

   (2) $\{x \mid -3 \le x \le 2\}$ (4) $\{x \mid x \le -2 \text{ or } x \ge 3\}$

3 The roots of a quadratic equation are *imaginary* when discriminant is

   (1) 0   (3) -16

   (2) 17   (4) 4

4 Which transformation is *not* an isometry?

   (1) $r_{y = x}$ (3) $R_{180°}$

   (2) D_{-3} (4) $T_{-2, 5}$

5 If $\cos x = \dfrac{5}{13}$, where $0 < x < 180°$, find the value of $\sin (180 - x)$

   (1) $\dfrac{5}{13}$ (3) $\dfrac{-5}{13}$

   (2) $\dfrac{12}{13}$ (4) $\dfrac{-12}{13}$

6 A rectangle fish pond is to be made larger. Its width is increased by 1 foot and it's length is increased by 2 feet. Its original length was 3 times its original width. If x represents the original width of the pond, which expression represents the difference between the new area and the original area?

   (1) $x^2 + 2x + 3$ (3) $5x + 2$

   (2) $3x^2$ (4) 6

7   Expressed in the simplest form, $i^{25} + i^5 - 4i^4 + i^{22}$ is equivalent to

(1) 1   (3) i

(2) -1   (4) -i

8   A function is defined by the equation $y = 3x + 7$. What equation defines the inverse of the function?

(1) $y = \dfrac{1}{3x + 7}$ (3) $x = \dfrac{1}{3y + 7}$

(2) $y = 3x - 7$ (4) $x = 3y + 7$

9   The speed of a gear varies inversely as the number of teeth. If a gear having 60 teeth makes 24 revolutions per minute, how many revolutions per minute will a gear with 20 teeth make?

(1) 8   (3) 50

(2) 48   (4) 56

10 For what integer value of x is the fraction undefined?

$$\frac{x^2 - 49}{x^2 - 2x + 1}$$

(1) $x = 1$ only   (3) $x = -1$ only

(2) $x = -1$ and $x = 1$ (4) $x = -7$ and $x = 7$

11 Express $306°$ in radian measure

(1) 1.7π (3) 0.85π

(2) 0.588   (4) 5.338

12 If $\log_x \dfrac{1}{25} = -2$, then x is

(1) 0.20   (3) 5.00

(2) 2.00   (4) 6.25

13 The graph of (10 - 5i) + (-2 + i) lies in what quadrant?

(1) 1   (3) 3

(2) 2   (4) 4

14 The graph of the equation $15(x - 3)^2 + 5(y - 9)^2 = 225$

(1) a circle with center (3, 9)   (3) a circle with radius of 15

(2) an ellipse with center (3, 9)   (4) a hyperbola in the 1st and 3rd quadrants

15 In a family of 5 children, what is the probability that there will be at most one male child?

(1) 15.625%   (3) 50%

(2) 18.75%   (4) 81.25%

16 What is the equation of the reflection of the graph of $y = -5 \cos 2x$ in the x axis?

(1) $y = -2 \cos 5x$ (3) $y = 5 \cos 2x$

(2) $y = \text{arc} \cos 5x$ (4) $y = 5 \sin 2x$

17 If $_nP_r$ represents the number of permutations of n things taken r at a time, what is the value of

$$\sum_{r=0}^{3} {}_5P_r \ ?$$

(1) 6   (3) 60

(2) 26   (4) 86

18 If $f(x) = x^2 + 1$ and $h(x) = x - 2$, which number satisfies

$$f(x) = (f \mathbf{o} h)(x) \ ?$$

(1) 1   (3) 3

(2) 2   (4) 4

19 Which diagram represents a one-to-one function?

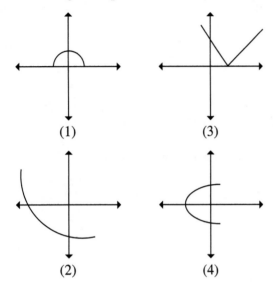

(1)   (3)

(2)   (4)

20 The graph of f(x) is shown in the accompanying diagram.

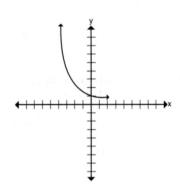

Which graph represents $f(x)_{r_{x\text{-axis}} \circ r_{y\text{-axis}}}$?

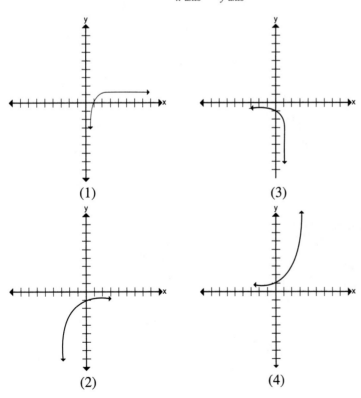

(1)   (3)

(2)   (4)

Part II

Answer all questions in this part. Each correct answer will receive 2 credits. Clearly indicate the necessary steps, including appropriate formula substitutions, diagrams, graphs, charts, etc. For all questions in this part, a correct numerical answer with no work shown will receive only 1 credit. [12]

21   250 people without diabetes were tested for blood glucose levels. The blood glucose levels are assumed to be normally distributed. The mean blood glucose level was found to be 90 milligrams per deciliter with a standard deviation of 10 mg/dL. How many people had a blood glucose level between 70 mg/dL and 110 mg/dL? Round your answer *down* to the nearest integer.

22   Two truck rental agencies are competing for the one day rental customer.
Company "R" charges $79 per day plus $0.29 per mile.
Company 'U" charges $20 per day plus $0.99 per mile.
Write an equation to find the number of miles where both companies charge the same amount/day. Solve your equation and round off to the *nearest mile*.

23   A stop sign is in the shape of a regular octagon. find the obtuse angle formed by two adjacent sides. Your answer must be in *degrees*.

24   If $\sin x = \dfrac{5}{13}$ and $\cos x$ is negative, find $\sin 2x$.

25   Show algebraically, without using numerical values, that

$$\frac{R_1 + R_2}{R_1 R_2} = \frac{1}{R_1} + \frac{1}{R_2}$$

Part II (continued)

26 A piece of property is in the shape of an isosceles triangle with one of the congruent sides equal to 150 feet. If the area of the property is 7071 square feet, find to the *nearest hundredth* of a degree, the three angles of the triangle.

Part III

Answer all questions in this part. Each correct answer will receive 4 credits. Clearly indicate the necessary steps, including appropriate formula substitutions, diagrams, graphs, charts, etc. For all questions in this part, a correct numerical answer with no work shown will receive only 1 credit. [24]

27 A store that sells automobile batteries determined that 1 out of 100 automobile batteries that it sells are returned because they are defective.
If 4 batteries selected at random, find the probability that
a *at least* 2 batteries selected are defective
b *at most* 2 batteries selected are defective
c *exactly* 2 batteries selected are defective

28 A barge is being pulled by two tugboats. One tugboat is pulling with force of 10 tons. The second barge is pulling with a force of 15 tons. The angle between the two tugboats forces is 20 degrees. Find the resultant force on the barge to the nearest ton.

29 An insurance company uses the following chart for advertising purposes

(x)	AGE	(years)	35	40	45	50	55
(y)	PREMIUM	($ per month)	16.9	21.87	34.56	56.00	83.56

Using a graphing calculator, find the slope and y-intercept of the linear regression line to the *nearest hundredth*.

Write the equation of the linear regression line using the slope and y-intercept found above.

Find the linear correlation coefficient to the *nearest thousandth*.

Using the 2-Var Stats of the graphing calculator, find $\bar{x}$, $\bar{y}$, *sample* standard deviation of x and *sample* standard deviation of y to the *nearest tenth*.

30 Solve for x: $\log_3(x^2 + 4x) - \log_3(x + 2) = 1$

31 Describe the composition of transformations performed on graph *a* to map onto graph *b*.

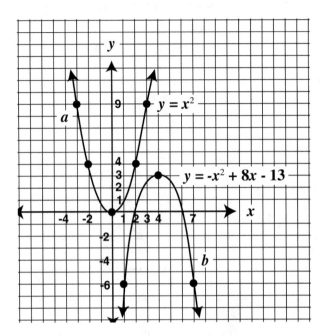

32 Point P lies outside circle O, which has a diameter $\overline{AOB}$. The angle formed by tangent $\overline{PA}$ and secant $\overline{PCB}$ measures 40°. Sketch the conditions given above and find the number of degrees in the measure of minor arcs AC and BC.

Part IV

33   A sine wave test generator in an electronics laboratory can delivery two sine wave signals to a prototype electronics circuit. The equations for the sine wave signals are know to be

$$y_1 = 4 \sin^2 x + 5 \qquad \text{and} \qquad y_2 = 8 - \sin x$$

Find all values of x, in *degrees*, for which the two sine wave signals meet in the interval $0° \leq x < 360°$ [Only an algebraic solution will be accepted.}

34   Given: chords $\overline{EB}$ and $\overline{TN}$ of circle O interest at X, an interior point of circle O and chords $\overline{EN}$ and $\overline{TB}$ are drawn.

Prove: a $\triangle$ NEX ~ $\triangle$ BTX

b $\overline{EX} : \overline{TX} = \overline{NX} : \overline{BX}$

c $(TX)(NX) = (EX)(BX)$

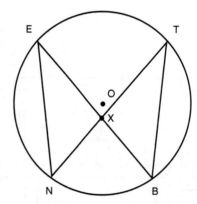

141

Scrap Graph Paper – This sheet will not be scored.

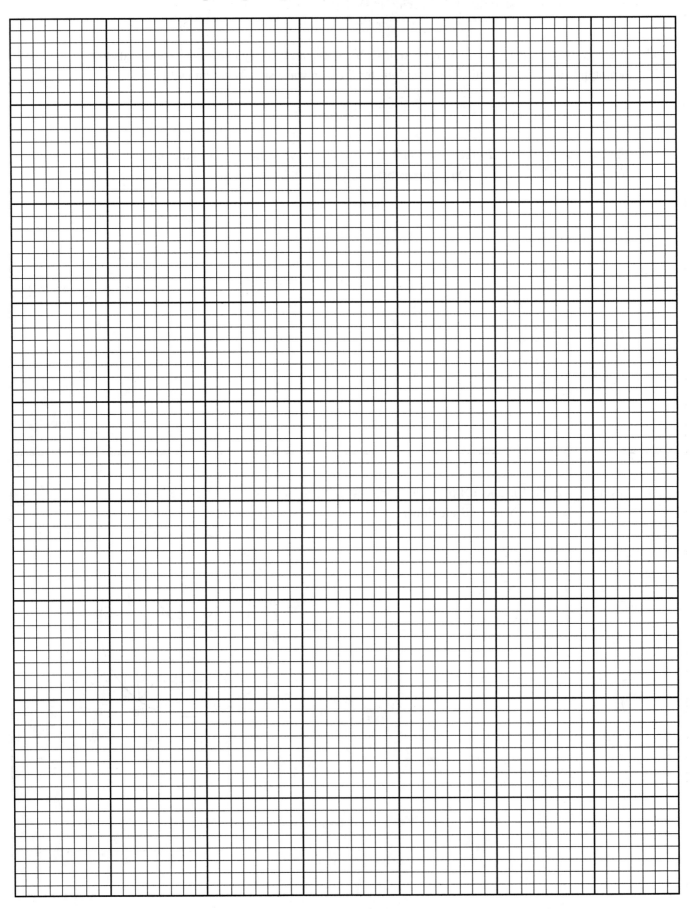

MATHEMATICS B

Practice Regents Exams

Answer Sheet

Pupil _____ Teacher _____

School _____ Grade _____

Your answers to Part I should be recorded on this answer sheet.

Part I

Answer all 20 questions in this part.

1 _____ 6 _____ 11 _____ 16 _____

2 _____ 7 _____ 12 _____ 17 _____

3 _____ 8 _____ 13 _____ 18 _____

4 _____ 9 _____ 14 _____ 19 _____

5 _____ 10 _____ 15 _____ 20 _____

Your answers to Part II, III, IV should be written on the paper provided by the school.

The declaration below should be signed when you have completed the examination.

I do hereby affirm, at the close of this examination, that I had no unlawful knowledge of the questions or answers prior to the examination, and that I have neither given nor received assistance in answering any of the questions during the examination.

_____
Signature

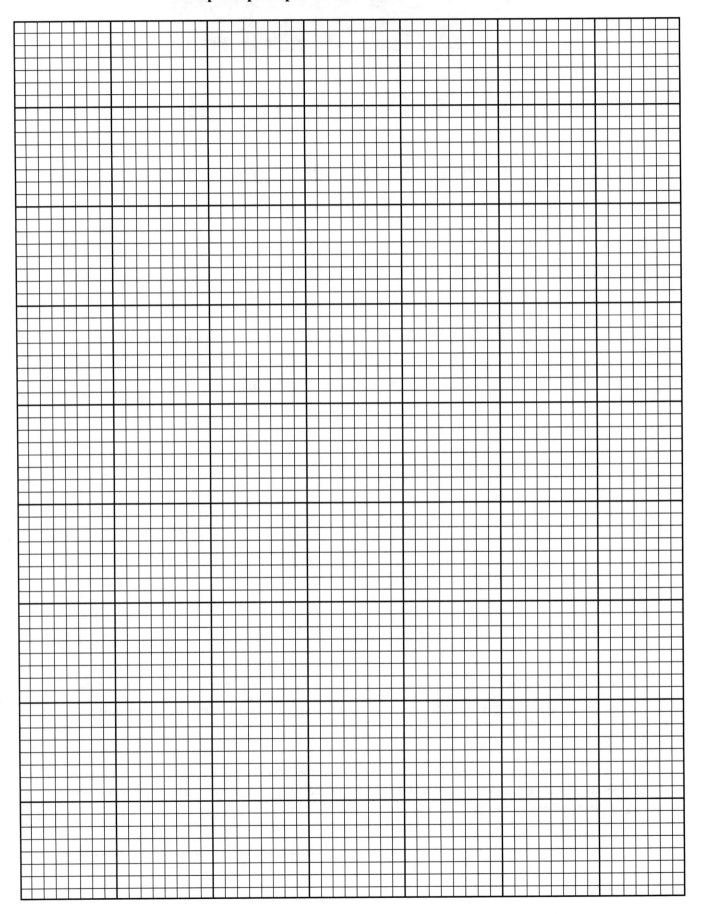

REGENTS HIGH SCHOOL
MATHEMATICS B

Exam Review Workbook

[Parts II, III and IV Students Constructed Response Questions]

EXTRA HELP

TABLE OF CONTENTS

UNIT 1 MATHEMATICAL REASONING

<u>**SEQUENTIAL MATHEMATICS 3**</u>

UNIT 2 NUMBER and NUMERATION

<u>**SEQUENTIAL MATHEMATICS 3**</u>

UNIT 3 OPERATIONS

<u>**SEQUENTIAL MATHEMATICS 3**</u>

UNIT 4 MODELING/MULTIPLE REPRESENTATION

<u>**SEQUENTIAL MATHEMATICS 3**</u>

UNIT 5 MEASUREMENT

<u>**SEQUENTIAL MATHEMATICS 3**</u>

TABLE OF CONTENTS (continued)

UNIT 6 UNCERTAINTY

UNIT 7 PATTERNS/FUNCTIONS

The following pages of SEQUENTIAL MATHEMATICS 3 are applicable to

MATHEMATICS B

Use of the TI-83 PLUS Graphing Calculator is shown.

SEQUENTIAL MATHEMATICS 3

Supplement for

REGENTS HIGH SCHOOL

MATHEMATICS

B Part I

[Using the TI-83 PLUS Graphing Calculator]

Exam Review Workbook
[Multiple-Choice Questions]

Formulas

Area of Triangle

$K = \frac{1}{2}ab \sin C$

Functions of the Sum of Two Angles

$\sin (A + B) = \sin A \cos B + \cos A \sin B$
$\cos (A + B) = \cos A \cos B - \sin A \sin B$

Functions of the Difference of Two Angles

$\sin (A - B) = \sin A \cos B - \cos A \sin B$
$\cos (A - B) = \cos A \cos B + \sin A \sin B$

Law of Sines

$\dfrac{a}{\sin A} = \dfrac{b}{\sin B} = \dfrac{c}{\sin C}$

Law of Cosines

$a^2 = b^2 + c^2 - 2bc \cos A$

Functions of the Double Angle

$\sin 2A = 2 \sin A \cos A$
$\cos 2A = \cos^2 A - \sin^2 A$
$\cos 2A = 2 \cos^2 A - 1$
$\cos 2A = 1 - 2 \sin^2 A$

Functions of the Half Angle

$\sin \frac{1}{2}A = \pm \sqrt{\dfrac{1 - \cos A}{2}}$

$\cos \frac{1}{2}A = \pm \sqrt{\dfrac{1 + \cos A}{2}}$

Normal Curve

Standard Deviation

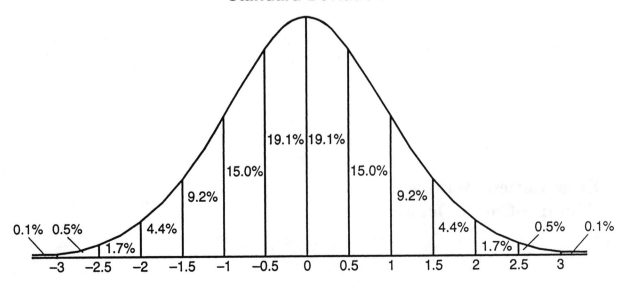

SEQUENTIAL MATH 3

Page 7   Direct Variation

$\dfrac{x_1}{x_2} = \dfrac{y_1}{y_2}$ Straight Line: $y = mx + b$ $(y_2 - y_1) = m(x_2 - x_1)$

m = slope, b = y-intercept

Example: Graph and find the point of intersection of: $y = 2x$ and $y = \dfrac{-x}{2}$

Solution: Press   **Y =** key

Enter functions under **Plot1**   \Y$_1$ = **2x**   Press **down cursor.**

\Y$_2$ = **-x/2**   Press **ENTER** key

Press **Zoom** key   Press **6** key which is Zoom Standard   Press **TRACE** key

Pressing the down or up cursor toggles between Y$_1$ = 2x and Y$_2$ = -x/2 label.

The two graphs are seen intersecting at point (0, 0).

Are the two graphs perpendicular? Justify your answer.

Page 8   Inverse Variation

$\dfrac{x_1}{x_2} = \dfrac{y_2}{y_1}$ Hyperbola: $xy > 0$ and $xy < 0$

Quad I, III   Quad II, IV

Example 1: Graph: $xy = 25$

Solution 1: Press   **Y =** key

Enter functions under **Plot1**   \Y$_1$ = **25/x**

Press **Zoom** key   Press **6** key which is Zoom Standard

Pressing the down/left or up/right cursor keys will allow you to read out coordinate points on the hyperbola. What are the asymptotes?

Example 2: Graph: $xy = -25$

Solutions 2: Repeat the steps in solution 1 above. If it did not work, did you use the subtraction key, —, instead of the negative key, (-)? What quadrants is the hyperbola in?

Page 9   Irrational Denominators

Example :   Simplify: $\dfrac{6}{5 + \sqrt{3}}$

Solution: Enter the following with no spaces: 6/(5+ $\sqrt{}$ (3)) Press ENTER

.8912588707   answer

SEQUENTIAL MATH 3

(Using the TI-83 PLUS Graphing Calculator)

Page 27   Quadratic Formula (real roots)

Example 1: Find the roots of the equation $2x^2 - 5x + 1 = 0$

Solution 1: Enter the coefficients 2, - 5, and 1 by pressing the following keys:

Press	**2**	**STO→**	**ALPHA**	**A**		**ALPHA**	**:**
	(–)	**5**	**STO→**	**ALPHA**	**B**	**ALPHA**	**:**
	1	**STO→**	**ALPHA**	**C**			

Now store the values to the variables A, B, and C:

Press   **ENTER**

Enter the expression for one of the solutions for the quadratic formula,

$(- B + \sqrt{(B^2 - 4AC)}) \div (2A)$

Press	**(**	**(–)**	**ALPHA**	**B**	**+**	**2nd**	**√**	**ALPHA**	**B**	**x²**
	– 4	**ALPHA**	**A**	**ALPHA**	**C**	**)**	**)**			
	÷ (	**2**	**ALPHA**	**A**	**)**					

Press   **ENTER**   to find one solution is 2.280776406

This is seen on the screen:

```
2→A: -5→B: 1→C
                  1
(-B+√ (B²-4AC)) / (
2A)
        2.280776406
```

To save keystrokes, recall the last expression you entered, and then edit it for the negative radical calculation.

Press	**2nd**	**ENTRY**	This recalls fraction conversion entry.
Press	**2nd**	**ENTRY**	This recalls the quadratic formula.
Press	↑		to move cursor onto the + sign in the formula.
Press	–		to edit the quadratic formula for the negative radical value.
Press	**ENTER**		to find the other solution **0.2192235936**

A-6

(Using the TI-83 PLUS Graphing Calculator)

Page 27   Quadratic Formula (imaginary roots)

Example 2: Find roots of the equation $2x^2 - 3x + 3 = 0$

Solution 2: When you set $a + bi$ complex number mode, the TI-83 PLUS
displays complex results.

Press	**MODE**				
Press	↓	6 times and → once to position the cursor over $a + bi$.			
Press	**ENTER** to select $a + bi$ complex number mode.				
Press	**2nd**	**QUIT**	to return to the home screen.		
Press	**CLEAR** to clear the home screen.				

Enter the coefficients 2, – 3, and 3 by pressing the following keys:

Press	2	STO→	ALPHA	A	ALPHA	:
	(–)	3	STO→	ALPHA B	ALPHA	:
	3	STO→	ALPHA	C		

Now store the values to the variables A, B, and C:

Press   **ENTER**

Enter the expression for one of the solutions for the quadratic formula,
$(-B + \sqrt{(B^2 - 4AC)}) \div (2A)$

Press	(	(–)	ALPHA	B	+	2nd	√	ALPHA	B	x²
	–	4	ALPHA	A	ALPHA	C	)	)		
	÷	(	2	ALPHA	A	)				

Press   **ENTER** to find one solution is $.75 + .9682458366i$

This is seen on the screen:

```
2→A: -3→B: 3→C
                      3
(-B+√(B²-4AC)) / (
2A)
 .75 + .9682458366i
```

Follow the last 5 step procedure on the prior page. The other solution is **.75 - .9682458366i**

Note that the two roots are *complex conjugates*.

SEQUENTIAL MATH 3

Page 56   Graphing $y = A \sin bx$

Example 1:   Graph the functions $y = \sin x + 4$

Solution 1:   Press **Y =** key.
               Enter functions under **Plot1**   \Y1 = sin (x) + 4
               Press **SIN** key   sin(
               Press **X** key   sin(x
               Press **)** key   sin(x)
               Press **+** key   sin(x) +
               Press **4** key   sin(x) + 4
               Press **Zoom** key Press **6** key   Zstandard

               The graph $y = \sin x + 4$ is displayed.

a   Using the *Vertical Line Test*, justify whether the graph is indeed a function.
b   What is the *amplitude*?
c   What is the *frequency*?
d   Using the formula: period = $\dfrac{2\pi \text{ radians}}{\text{frequency}}$, calculate the *period in radians*.

e   Using the formula: period = $\dfrac{360^{\circ}}{\text{frequency}}$, calculate the *period in degrees*.

d   Move the cursor left/right for $x = 0$. Now move the cursor up/down and read the value of y.

e   Why doesn't the graph cross the x - axis?

f   Is the graph shown in quadrant I reflected over the y-axis to quadrant II? Explain

Example 2: Repeat example 1 above for: $y = \dfrac{1}{2} \sin 2x + 4$

Page 57   Graphing $y = A \cos bx$

Example 3:   Repeat example 1 above for $y = \cos x + 4$

Example 4:   Repeat example 1 above for: $y = \dfrac{1}{2} \cos 2x + 4$

SEQUENTIAL MATH 3

(Using the TI-83 PLUS Graphing Calculator)

Page 59   Fractional Exponents

Example: If $f(x) = x^{\frac{3}{2}} - 3x^0 + 9x^{-1}$, find f (9).

Solution: Enter the following information. The following will be seen in the calculator display:

     9 ^ (3/2) - 3(9) ^ 0 + 9   [Note: $- 3x^0$ use subtraction - key

     (9) ^ - 1 $9x^{-1}$ use negative sign (-) key]

                25   answer

Page 66 Law of Sines   **[MODE Normal Degree]**

$\dfrac{\text{side a}}{\sin A} = \dfrac{\text{side b}}{\sin B}$ If a = 8, m $\angle$ A = 12°, and b = 10, find $\angle$ B to the *nearest degree*.

$\dfrac{8}{\sin 12^{\circ}} = \dfrac{10}{\sin B}$ m $\angle$ B = $\sin^{-1}$ B = $\sin^{-1} \dfrac{10 \sin 12^{\circ}}{8}$

Press **2nd SIN** $\sin^{-1}($

Press **10**   Press **X**   Press **SIN** $\sin^{-1}(10 * \sin($

Press **1**   Press **2**   Press **)** $\sin^{-1}(10 * \sin(12)$

Press **÷**   Press **8**   Press **)** $\sin^{-1}(10 * \sin(12)/8)$

Press **ENTER**   15.0635123   answer 15°

Page 67 Law of Cosines

$c^2 = a^2 + b^2 - 2ab \cos C$ If a = 14, b = 20, and c = 16, find m $\angle$C to the *nearest degree*.

$16^2 = 14^2 + 20^2 - 2(14)(20) \cos C$

m $\angle$ C = $\cos^{-1}$ C = $\cos^{-1} \dfrac{16^2 - 14^2 - 20^2}{-2(14)(20)}$

Press **2nd   COS** $\cos^{-1}($

Press **(**   Press **16 ^ 2 - 14 ^ 2 - 20 ^ 2** $\cos^{-1}((16 \wedge 2 - 14 \wedge 2 - 20 \wedge 2$

Press **)**   Press **÷** Press **(** $\cos^{-1}((16 \wedge 2 - 14 \wedge 2 - 20 \wedge 2)/($

Press **-2(14)(20)))** $\cos^{-1}((16 \wedge 2 - 14 \wedge 2 - 20 \wedge 2)/(-2(14)(20)))$

Press **ENTER**   52.61680158   answer 53°

SEQUENTIAL MATH 3

(Using the TI-83 PLUS Graphing Calculator)

Page 68   Area of a Triangle

Example: Two sides of a triangle are 12 and 30. The included angle measures 150°.

Find the area of the triangle to the *nearest integer*.

$K = \dfrac{1}{2}$ ab sin C $= \dfrac{1}{2}(12)(30) \sin 150^{\circ}$ **[MODE   Normal   Degree]**

Enter: **1 ÷ 2 (12) (30) SIN 150)**   1/2 (12)(30)sin(150)

Press **ENTER**   90   answer 90°

Page 71   Solving Trigonometric Equations

Example: Solve for all values of Θ in the interval $0^{\circ} < \Theta \leq 360^{\circ}$

$2\cos^2 \Theta + \cos \Theta = 1$

Solution: Let $x = \cos \Theta$ then $x^2 = \cos^2 \Theta$

$2x^2 + x = 1$ For practice, let's *assume that it can not be factored* as $(x + 1)(2x - 1)$ and we want to use the quadratic formula.

Refer to page A6 with the heading "Page 27   Quadratic Formula (real roots)".
We find $x = -1$ and $x = 0.5$
Therefore, $\cos \Theta = -1$ where $\Theta = 180^{\circ}$ and
              $\cos \Theta = 0.5$ where Θ is positive in quadrants I and IV
$\cos^{-1} (.5) = 60^{\circ}$ quadrant I and $360^{\circ} - 60^{\circ} = 300^{\circ}$ quadrant IV
[Note: Depending on the quadrant the angle is in, add or subtract the acute angle to or from 180° or 360°. Do not use 90° or 270°.] answer $60^{\circ}, 180^{\circ}, 300^{\circ}$

Page 82   Conjugate, Multiplicative Inverse, Additive Inverse

Example: Given the complex number: 8 - 2i

a   Use the **MATH** key and move the → cursor key 2 times to **CPX**.

    1: conj(Press   **1**   conj(**8 - 2i**)   Press **ENTER**   answer   8 + 2i

    2: real(Press   **2**   real(**8 - 2i**)   Press **ENTER**   answer   8

    3: imag(Press   **3**   imag(**8 - 2i**)   Press **ENTER**   answer   -2

    4: angle(Press   **4**   angle(**8 - 2i**)   Press **ENTER**   answer -14.03624347°

    5: abs(Press   **5**   abs(**8 - 2i**)   Press **ENTER**   answer   8.24621125

         [Do you know how to find the same answer using $a^2 + b^2 = c^2$ for 5: abs(?]

(Using the TI-83 PLUS Graphing Calculator)

Page 82   Conjugate Multiplicative Inverse, Additive Inverse (continued)

b Find *Multiplicative Inverse* of 8 - 2i.

Solution; enter into the graphing calculator: **1/(8 - 2i)**

  Press **Enter**   .1176470588 + .0294117647i   answer

c Find the *Additive Inverse* of 8 - 2i

Solution: Just multiply by - 1 using the distributive property.

    -1(8 - 2i) = -8 + 2i   answer

Page 85   Mode, Median, Mean, Range, Standard Deviation

Example: Given the data: 55, 60, 75, 80, 80, 85, 90

Solution: MODE is the data that appears the most times.   answer 80

    MEDIAN is the middle piece of data after they are
        arranged in order. If there are an even
        number of pieces of data, average the two
        middle values,   answer 80

    MEAN the arithmetic mean or average.

$$\overline{X} = \frac{\sum \text{data}}{n} = \frac{55 + 60 + 75 + 2(80) + 85 + 90}{7}$$ answer $\overline{X} = 75$

List [use 2nd STAT]. Move cursor to the right to highlight MATH
Press **3** to select mean(
After mean(type in **{55,60,75,80,85,90},{1,1,1,2,1,1}**)   {Note the set brackets}
Press **ENTER**   answer 75

RANGE = MAX - MIN = 90 - 55 = 35   answer 35

STANDARD DEVIATION:
LIST [use 2nd STAT]. Move cursor to the right to highlight MATH
Press **7** to select stdDev(
After StdDev(type in **{55,60,75,80,85,90},{1,1,1,2,1,1}**)
Press **ENTER**   answer 12.9099449

SEQUENTIAL MATH 3

(Using the TI-83 PLUS Graphing Calculator)

Page 127   Miscellaneous problems

Example 1: Find $\dfrac{\sqrt[3]{1370}}{5}$ to the *nearest hundredth*.

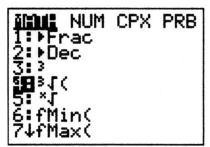

Solution 1:   Press **MODE** key
Move cursor to highlight
2 decimal places
Press **ENTER** key
Press **MATH** key
Press **4** key
Type in **1370)/5**
Press **ENTER** key

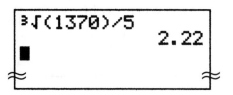

An alternative method
Press **CLEAR** key
Type in **(1370 ^ (1/3))/5**
Press **ENTER** key

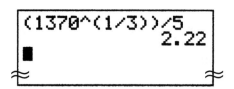

Example 2: Find *x* to the *nearest tenth*.

$$4^x = 19$$

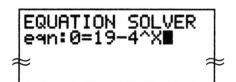

Solution 2:

Using **EQUATION SOLVER**
in the graphing calculator, first
set the equation = 0

Press the **MODE** key for 1 decimal place.
Press **MATH** key
Press   **0**   key for EQUATION SOLVER
Type in **19-4^X** or equivalent
Press **ENTER** key

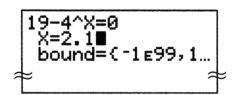

An alternative method:
You know that *x* is between 2 and 3.
Type in **4^2.1** and Press **ENTER.**
Type in **4^2.2** and Press **ENTER**

Select *x* where 4^x is closest to 19.

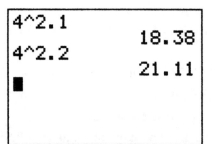

SEQUENTIAL MATH 3

(Using the TI-83 PLUS Graphing Calculator)

Page 120   Graphing Trigonometric Functions

Example 1: Graph $y = 2\sin(x)$

using a *standard* solid line

and

$y = 2\cos(x)$

using a *thick* solid line.

Solution 1:

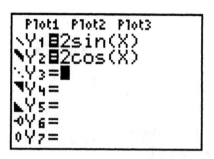

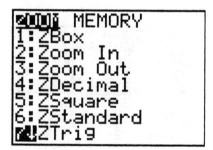

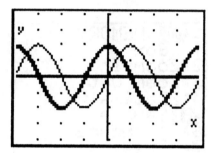

Example 2: Graph $y \geq 2\sin(x)$

using the *above graph* style

and

$y \leq 2\cos(x)$

using the *below graph* style.

Solution 2:

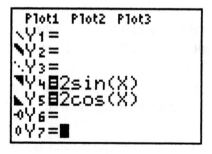

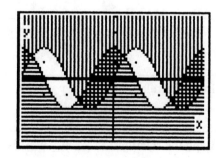

The icon for **Y₃** graphs the function as a *dotted* line.

The icon for **Y₆** causes a circular cursor to trace the leading edge of the graph and *draw a path*.

The icon for **Y₇** causes a circular cursor to trace the leading edge of the graph *without drawing a path*.

SEQUENTIAL MATH 3

(Using the TI-83 PLUS Graphing Calculator)

Page 129   Graphing Two Variable Inequalities

Example: Graph $y \geq 2x^2 - 4x + 1$

                using the *above graph* style

                and

                $y \leq -2x + 5$

                using the *below graph* style.

Solution:

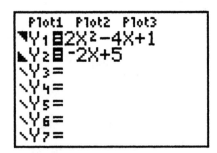

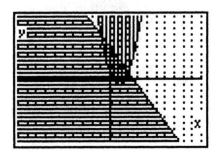

Use the cursor keys to position the cursor over the \ symbol in front of y_1. The \ fluctuates $45°$.
Toggle the **ENTER** key until you see the *above graph* style right triangle in front of y_1.

Use the cursor keys to position the cursor over the \ symbol in front of y_2. The \ fluctuates $45°$.
Toggle the **ENTER** key until you see the *below graph* style right triangle in front of y_2.

Type in $2x^2 - 4x + 1$ for y_1 and type in $-2x + 5$ for y_2. Do *not* leave any spaces.
Press the **ZOOM** key and press **5** for ZSquare. The two inequalities will graph as shown above.
The solution set is the area of overlap as seen in the graph above.

---

1. Graph the relations: $x^2 + y^2 \leq 25$ and $x - y \geq 1$ Hint: Use **VARS** key, >
                                                      Y-VARS, 1:Function, press no.

---

2. Graph the relations: $y \leq -2x^2 - 4x + 2$ and $2x \leq y - 2$ Hint: ÷ by a negative or
                                                × by a negative reverses inequality.

---

3. Graph the relations: $y \leq x^2 - 3x - 10$ and $3x - y \geq 19$

---

4. Graph the relations: $x^2 + y^2 \geq 25$ and $x \leq y - 1$
